Deliciously Irish

A collection of recipes
from the
hosts and chefs
of Ireland

by

Viki Pidgeon

Rosina,
If you're lucky enough to be
Irish... you're lucky enough!

Viki Pidgeon

International Standard Book Number 0-9747171-0-X
Library of Congress Card Catalog Number 2003098382

Cover design and book layout by James Asher Graphics

Manufactured in the United States of America

All book order correspondence should be addressed to:

Pidgeon's Press
8318 Aiken Rd.
Louisville, KY 40245

email: Pidgeonspress@aol.com

Dedication

Deliciously Irish is dedicated to the kind people of Ireland, who were gracious enough to share a few of their favorite recipes with me. Without their generosity this cookbook would not have become a reality. Their patience in answering questions in reference to the recipes is greatly appreciated, as well. I would so enjoy meeting and thanking each and everyone personally, rather than the few that I have been fortunate enough to meet.

Acknowledgements

On the very day I decided to compile an Irish cookbook I envisioned Michael Kennedy's pottery on the cover; never did I consider contacting another artist. The day I received the news from Michael that he would, indeed, feature his beautiful pottery on the front cover was the day everything seemed to fall into place.

Thanks to my husband Barney for sending me off with a kiss and a smile when I left on my trip to Ireland in March of 2002. It was during this holiday that I hatched my **Deliciously Irish** cookbook idea.

Table of Contents

Traditional Irish Breakfast

The Irish believe in starting the day off with a filling, stick to your ribs, traditional "Irish Breakfast." It's definitely not a "low fat, low cholesterol, healthy heart" breakfast. Generally, one starts out with a small bowl of fruit, a bowl of cereal or both along with a cup of tea, which would be more than enough for most people. No sooner have you taken your last bite where upon lifting your eyes to take a sip of tea you see the "Full Irish" arriving, taking the place of your empty fruit and cereal bowls. A traditional Irish breakfast or a "Full Irish," as it is so often referred to, includes the following: a few slices of Irish bacon (which is similar to what Americans know as Canadian bacon), a couple pork sausages (link type), slices of black and white pudding, fried mushrooms, an egg or two (fried unless you request differently), 1 small tomato, halved, and broiled, homemade brown and white soda breads and, of course, more tea. By the time you have consumed your "Full Irish" you have had more than enough food to carry you through a busy day of sightseeing.

French Toast
à la Carolans

8

¼ cup milk
⅓ cup Carolans Irish Cream
¼ cup milk
4 eggs, well beaten
⅛ teaspoon almond extract
Butter
12 slices French bread
Toasted almonds
Powdered sugar

In a shallow bowl mix milk, Carolans Irish Cream, eggs and almond extract. Melt butter in a large skillet. Dip French bread in egg mixture, coating both sides. Cook in butter until both sides are golden brown. Serve immediately with toasted almonds and powdered sugar.

Makes 4 three-slice servings.

Carolans Irish Cream Liqueur
Clonmel
Co. Tipperary

Crepes Eugene

2 cups all-purpose flour
4 eggs
1 cup milk
1 cup water
½ teaspoon salt
3 tablespoons butter, melted
1 tablespoon orange zest
Few drops of vegetable oil
4 ounces unsalted butter
4 teaspoons extra fine sugar
1 teaspoon light honey
Juice of 1 orange
3 fluid ounces Irish Mist Liqueur
Orange slices (optional)
Fresh mint (optional)

Mix flour and eggs together. Add milk, water, salt and melted butter and mix until smooth; add orange zest and oil to the batter. Allow batter to rest at least one hour. Make 4 crepes. Fold each finished crepe in half then in half again. Put on a platter. In a sauté pan, melt unsalted butter. Sprinkle sugar into pan and allow sugar to melt until near caramelization. Do not stir sugar while it is melting. Add honey and orange juice and let boil, stirring occasionally. Spoon syrup over folded crepes. Add Irish Mist and flame it. Garnish with orange slices and fresh mint.

Irish Mist
Tullamore
Co. Offaly

Poached Plums

10

1 cup water
1 tablespoon honey
½ teaspoon cinnamon
4 well-ripened plums
Natural yogurt

Put water, honey and cinnamon in a saucepan and bring to a boil. Cut plums in quarters and add to boiling water, cover and simmer for 2 minutes then remove from the heat and leave to cool overnight. Serve with natural yogurt.

Sea Shore Farm
Guesthouse
Tubrid, Kenmare
Co. Kerry

Temple Spa Orange Semolina Soufflés

5 large juicy oranges
2 tablespoons sugar
1 ounce semolina flour or rice flour
3 eggs, separated
Confectioner's sugar for dusting

Finely grate the rind and squeeze the juice from 2 of the oranges. You will need 1 cup of juice. Make up the juice from one of the remaining oranges, if necessary. Halve the remaining oranges. Cut out orange segments and any loose flesh. Cut a thin slice from each of the 6 halves so that they stand flat. Place the orange juice and rind, sugar and flour in a pan and simmer until thickened, stirring all the time. Cool slightly then stir in the egg yolks. Whisk the egg whites until stiff and fold into the mixture. Spoon mixture into the orange shells and place on a baking sheet. Bake at 400 degrees for 15-20 minutes or until risen and golden brown. Dust with confectioner's sugar and serve.

Temple Health Spa
Horseleap, Moate
Co. Westmeath

McCann's Oatmeal Pancakes

12

*McCann's quick cooking oatmeal can be found in many grocery stores and specialty stores as well as some Irish shops.

1¼ cups of McCann's quick cooking oatmeal*
1 cup plain yogurt
1 cup low-fat milk
1 teaspoon honey or sugar
¼ cup all-purpose white flour
¼ cup whole wheat flour
1 teaspoon baking soda
1 teaspoon salt
2 large eggs, beaten
¼ cup chopped walnuts
Maple syrup
Fresh Fruit (optional)

In a large bowl combine McCann's Quick Cooking Oatmeal, plain yogurt, low-fat milk and honey. Stir in flour, baking soda and salt. Add beaten eggs and mix well. Add chopped walnuts. Batter will be thick. Heat a large nonstick skillet or griddle over medium heat. Spoon ¼ cup batter onto a hot griddle for each pancake. Cook until bottoms are browned and bubbles on top start to pop, about 3 minutes. Flip and cook until other sides are browned, about 2 minutes. Repeat with remaining batter. Add additional milk if batter becomes too thick. Serve with hot maple syrup and/or fresh fruit.

**McCann's Irish Oatmeal
Sallins
Co. Kildare**

Makes 12 pancakes – 4 servings.

Breads, Scones, & Muffins

Ballinadee Brown Bread

14

3¼ cups brown whole wheat flour
½ cup all-purpose flour
¼ cup wheat germ
¼ cup bran
1 ounce linseeds
1 teaspoon baking soda
1 teaspoon salt
1 teaspoon sugar
1½ cups buttermilk
1 egg, beaten
Dash of olive oil

Preheat oven to 350 degrees. Mix wet ingredients into dry. Pour into a 2-pound oiled bread pan. Bake for approximately 55 minutes.

Glebe Country House
Ballinadee, Bandon
Co. Cork

Citrus Tea Bread

15

2 teaspoons Earl Grey tea, loose tea
½ cup boiling water
½ stick butter
¾ cup sugar
1 egg, lightly beaten
1 tablespoon grated orange rind
1 teaspoon grated lemon rind
3 cups flour
1 teaspoon baking powder
1 teaspoon baking soda
½ teaspoon salt
½ teaspoon cinnamon
¾ cup orange juice
½ cup chopped walnuts

Preheat oven to 350 degrees. Lightly grease a 9x4½-inch loaf pan. Mix tea with boiling water. Leave tea to steep for 3 minutes then strain. Cream the butter with the sugar until light and fluffy. Add egg and rinds and beat well. Sift flour, baking powder, baking soda, salt and cinnamon and add to butter mixture. Then stir in the tea and orange juice, and add nuts. Put mixture into prepared loaf pan and bake on the center shelf of the oven for 40 minutes.

Riverville House
Tubrid, Kenmare
Co. Kerry

Farmhouse Wheaten Bread

16

1¾ cups all-purpose flour
1¾ cups whole wheat flour
2 teaspoons baking soda
Pinch of salt
½ cup wheat germ
½ cup bran
¾ cup oatmeal
1 ounce sugar
1½ tablespoons honey
2 eggs
2 cups buttermilk

Preheat oven to 400 degrees. Grease 2 bread pans with butter then line with nonstick baking paper. Sift flours and baking soda together. Mix all of the dry ingredients together. Make a well in the center. Add honey, eggs and buttermilk to make a soft dough. Knead very little. Put into bread pans. Bake for 30-35 minutes until risen and nicely browned. Turn bread upside down while still in bread pans and place upside down on the middle rack of the oven for another 5 minutes. Remove from oven and wrap in a damp tea towel.

"Carrig-Gorm"
Helen's Bay, Bangor
Co. Down

Irish Soda Bread

2¾ cups white flour
1 cup whole wheat flour
1 teaspoon baking soda
1 teaspoon sugar
Pinch of salt
14 ounces buttermilk

17

Preheat oven to 400 degrees. Sift the flours and baking soda, making sure there are no lumps in the baking soda. Mix in the sugar and salt, making a well in the bottom of the bowl. Add almost all of the buttermilk in one go, mixing quickly and only just enough to make the ingredients come together in a manageable ball of dough. Add the rest of the milk if too dry. This is best done with your hands, or a knife, not a wooden spoon. Lift the dough out of the bowl and shape into a round on a baking sheet sprinkled with flour. Cut the dough (almost) into quarters and prick each quarter a couple of times. Bake for approximately 40 minutes. When cooked it will sound hollow when tapped on its bottom.

"You can make an entirely white loaf, or an entirely brown one, some people prefer a hotter oven for a crustier loaf — it's up to you, so experiment! You can add fruit or herbs, leave out the sugar, even use ordinary milk if you've got no buttermilk."

David

Iskeroon
Bunavalla, Caherdaniel
Co. Kerry

Irish Walnut Bread

18

3½ cups whole wheat flour*
1¾ cups all-purpose flour
1 heaping teaspoon baking soda
1 teaspoon salt
1 teaspoon sugar
2 eggs
2 cups buttermilk
1 cup yogurt
6 ounces treacle (molasses)
1 cup walnuts, chopped

If whole-wheat flour is very fine use 5 cups of whole meal flour and omit the all-purpose flour.

Preheat oven to 350 degrees and oil 2 loaf pans. Mix all dry ingredients together. Add eggs, buttermilk and yogurt. Warm treacle and walnuts together in a saucepan and mix with other ingredients. Put mixture into 2 loaf pans. Bake for 45 minutes.

Zetland Country
House Hotel
Cashel Bay, Connemara
Co. Galway

Margaret Browne's Brown Bread

19

3¼ cups whole wheat stone-ground flour
½ cup all-purpose flour
1 teaspoon salt
2 teaspoons brown sugar
1 tablespoon bran
1 teaspoon baking soda
14 ounces buttermilk
2 tablespoons cooking oil
1 egg, beaten

Preheat oven to 400 degrees. Mix all dry ingredients together, except baking soda. Sift baking soda into dry ingredients and mix in. Mix buttermilk, oil and egg together; add to dry ingredients. Spoon mixture into 2 greased loaf pans. Bake for 50-60 minutes.

Ballymakeigh House
Killeagh, Youghal
Co. Cork

McCann's Oatmeal Banana Bread

20

5 tablespoons butter
1 cup sugar
1 egg
1 cup mashed banana
1 cup flour
½ cup McCann's Quick Cooking Oatmeal
2 teaspoons baking powder
½ teaspoon salt
¼ cup chopped walnuts
¼ cup candied citrus peel

Preheat oven to 350 degrees. Cream the butter and sugar. Add the egg and mix well, beating all the time. Mix in the mashed banana. Combine the flour, oatmeal, baking powder and salt. Add this to the creamed mixture and stir well. Add the nuts and the candied peel. Spread the mixture into a greased loaf pan (approximately 10x5x2½ inches). Bake for about 45 minutes. Insert a skewer into the center of the bread – if it comes out clean the bread is cooked. When the bread is cool, put the bread on a wire tray and cover with a tea towel.

McCann's Irish Oatmeal
Sallins
Co. Kildare

Wheaten Bread

12 ounces course whole meal flour
6 ounces soda bread flour
1 ounce demerara sugar*
1 teaspoon baking soda
⅓ cup pinhead oatmeal*
2 cups buttermilk
2 tablespoons butter
3 ounces sunflower seeds (optional)

21

Preheat oven to 400 degrees. Place whole meal flour, bread flour, sugar, baking soda and half of the pinhead oatmeal into a large bowl and mix well. Add the buttermilk gradually and stir to a soft dough. Warm loaf pan and grease with butter. Turn the dough into a 8½x4½-inch loaf pan, cover with the remaining pinhead oatmeal and press in lightly with fingertips. Bake in oven at 400 degrees for the first 30 minutes, then at 350 degrees for a further 30 minutes. Turn out onto a wire rack to cool. The cooked bread should have a hollow sound when tapped on the base.

Demerara sugar is available in the health food section of many grocery stores as well as health food stores.

Pinhead oatmeal is available from McCann's Irish Oatmeal.

"Just give this lovely wheaten bread a different twist by adding 3 ounces of sunflower seeds to the mixture."
Sincere regards
Nora.

Nora teaches and runs a "cook school" four or five times each year.

Grange Lodge
Moy, Dungannon
Co. Tyrone

Breakfast Scones

4 cups self-rising flour
1 pinch salt
1 teaspoon baking powder
4 tablespoons margarine
4 tablespoons superfine sugar
4 tablespoons golden raisins
2 beaten eggs
1¼ cups cream

Maria's Schoolhouse is a beautiful old stone building and was featured in the January-February 2003 issue of "Ireland of the Welcomes Magazine."

Preheat oven to 400 degrees. Mix flour, salt and baking powder, rub in margarine. Add sugar and raisins to mixture. Add eggs and cream, (save a little cream and egg to brush on tops). When just mixed together turn out onto floured board, shape gently into a round approximately ¾-1-inch thick. Using a 2½ inch scone cutter cut into rounds and place onto a baking sheet. Brush tops with a little leftover cream and egg mixture. Bake for 20 minutes.

Makes 12-14 scones.

Maria's Schoolhouse
Union Hall
West Cork

Cheese Scones

23

3½ cups self-rising flour
1 stick margarine
1 cup grated cheese
1 egg
Milk

Preheat oven to 400 degrees. Mix ingredients, adding enough milk to make a soft dough. Roll out and cut with a small round pastry cutter. Place on a greased baking sheet. Bake in a hot oven for about 20 minutes.

Makes 12 scones.

Newpark House
Ennis
Co. Clare

Irish Tea-Brack

24

1 pound mixed fruit
(raisins, currants, golden raisins)
2 ounces chopped candied cherries
2 ounces mixed nuts
1 teaspoon ground ginger
1 teaspoon allspice
1 cup soft brown sugar
1 cup cold tea
1 egg, beaten
2 cups self-rising flour

Preheat oven to 350 degrees. Put the fruit, nuts, spices, sugar and tea in a bowl and leave for 3 hours or until the tea is absorbed. Beat in the egg and flour. Pour into a lined and greased 2-pound loaf pan and bake for 1½ -2 hours. Leave in the loaf pan for 5 minutes, and then cool on a wire rack. Serve sliced with butter.

Makes one 2-pound loaf.

The Quay House
Clifden
Co. Galway

Apple & Ginger Muffins

7 cups all-purpose flour
3 teaspoons ground nutmeg
4 eggs
¾ cup sunflower oil
2 apples, chopped or grated
8 ounces crystallized ginger, chopped
Milk
Honey, enough to brush the tops of muffins

Preheat oven to 425 degrees. Sift flour and nutmeg. Add eggs, sunflower oil, apples and ginger. If mixture is dry add a little milk – the mixture should be stiff. Place muffin liners into muffin pan and divide mix equally – normally makes 24. Bake 20-30 minutes. Test with a skewer. After removing from oven brush with a little honey while muffins are still hot.

Cleevaun Country House
Milltown, Dingle
Co. Kerry

Strawberry Muffins

26

4 ounces superfine sugar
1¾ cups all-purpose flour
Pinch of salt
1 teaspoon baking powder
6 tablespoons butter
3 tablespoons strawberry jam
½ cup strawberry yogurt
½ cup milk
1 egg

Preheat oven to 400 degrees. Sift all the dry ingredients together. Melt the butter and the jam; beat in the yogurt, milk and egg. Gently stir wet mixture into dry ingredients. Fill muffin tins three-quarters of the way full with mixture. Bake for 20 minutes, until well-risen and golden brown.

Old Weir Lodge
Killarney
Co. Kerry

Easter Biscuits

3½ cups all-purpose flour
1 teaspoon salt
1 teaspoon allspice
2 sticks butter, at room temperature
1 cup superfine sugar
2 large eggs, beaten
¾ cup currants
2 ounces candied peel, chopped
Milk, as required
Granulated sugar to sprinkle over

Preheat oven to 400 degrees. Sift flour, salt and allspice together. Cream butter and sugar until fluffy. Beat in the eggs and add alternately the currants and peel. Mix to a stiff dough, adding a little milk. Make a ball with the dough. Wrap in a plastic wrap and chill for at least one hour. Flour a work surface and roll out dough thinly. Prick all over with a fork and cut into rounds with a large cutter. Place rounds on a greased baking sheet leaving room between them. Bake 15-20 minutes until they are beginning to brown. Remove from oven and brush quickly with milk and sprinkle with granulated sugar. Return to oven for a few minutes until crisp and golden. Cool on baking sheet for 5 minutes and then transfer to a wire rack. When biscuits are cooled store in an airtight container.

Carrigeen Castle
Cahir
Co. Tipperary

Flakemeal Biscuits

28

2 sticks margarine
½ cup superfine sugar
Pinch of salt
10 ounces flakemeal (porridge oats)
⅔+ cup flour
Pinch of baking soda

Preheat oven to 350 degrees. Cream margarine and sugar together; add dry ingredients. Roll out and cut into biscuits. Bake for about 20 minutes.

Ardeen B&B
Ramelton
Co. Donegal

Starters, Salads & Others

Asparagus Mousse

30

1 pound fresh asparagus
1 handful of herbs (parsley, chives, fennel)
Salt and pepper
1½ cups cream
3 eggs
2 egg yolks

* Refresh asparagus by plunging them in ice water to arrest the cooking process.

* Bain-marie is a term for a cooking technique we know as water bath. It consists of placing a baking pan, bowl, ramekins, etc. of food in a large, shallow pan of warm water, which surrounds the food.

Cook and refresh* asparagus. Chop up herbs in a food processor. Add asparagus, salt and pepper and cream to food processor. Taste, as you may need to add more salt as this mousse takes quite a bit. Add the eggs and egg yolks. Spoon the mousse into ramekins and place them in a bain-marie* with a tight fitting foil lid. Place in the oven at 350 degrees for 40 minutes. Turn mousse out onto plates and drizzle the White Wine Sauce over the top.

Makes 6-8 mousses depending upon the size of the ramekins.

White Wine Sauce

⅔ cup vegetable stock
⅔ cup white wine
½ cup cream
Salt and pepper to taste

31

Combine the vegetable stock and white wine and reduce to a couple of tablespoons. Add cream and salt and pepper to taste. Reduce the sauce by half.

"The wonderful real garden green of this mousse looks fabulous in white ramekins on white dinner plates with the white wine sauce drizzled over the plate."

Emma Hewlett

Kilmokea
Great Island, Campile
Co. Wexford

Killeen House Hotel's Salsa

This warm salad goes well with the Oven Roasted Rack of Lamb on a Garlic Mash with a Pesto Fondue on page 74.

12 cherry tomatoes, halved
4 onion shallots, finely chopped
2 cloves garlic, finely chopped
1 cup olive oil
1 tablespoon dried mixed herbs
10 black olives, pitted and halved
1 cup balsamic vinegar
Salt and pepper to taste

Combine all ingredients together in a baking dish. Place in a 375-degree oven and bake for 15 minutes.

Killeen House Hotel
Lakes of Killarney
Co. Kerry

Rhubarb & Orange Chutney

4 oranges
3 pounds rhubarb, cut into 1-inch lengths
1 pound onions, chopped
1 pound raisins
3 cups malt vinegar
1½ pounds brown sugar
1 teaspoon ground mace
1 teaspoon ground cinnamon
1 teaspoon ground allspice

Remove rind from oranges. Cut away and discard the white pith. Chop the flesh and remove the pips. Reserve juice. Put juice and flesh with remainder of ingredients in a non-reactive saucepan and bring to a boil and let simmer for 2½ hours until mixture is thick and dark, stirring carefully to make sure mixture does not stick. Store in sterilized jars (about five or six, 1-pound jars) and seal immediately. Keep one month before using. Once opened eat within 3 weeks. Unopened and carefully cooked and stored in sterilized jars it will keep up to two years.

Park Hotel Kenmare
Kenmare
Co. Kerry

Hot Chicken Mousse

34

¾ pound chicken breast fillets
3 tablespoons butter, divided
Salt and pepper
3 red peppers
1½ ounces chopped onion
2 egg whites, refrigerated
1 cup heavy cream
¼ teaspoon marjoram
Pinch of nutmeg
Salt and pepper
½ cup sour cream
½ teaspoon paprika
Watercress or parsley for garnish

Cut chicken fillets into small pieces and fry quickly in 1 tablespoon butter. Season with salt and pepper, let cool 1 hour. Cut peppers in half, remove cores and seeds; heat in oven or under grill for 10 minutes, until the skins have black patches on them. Remove from the heat, cover with foil for 5 minutes and then remove the skins. Cook onions in 1 tablespoon butter. Allow to cool, then place in the refrigerator until well chilled. Blend the cooled chicken meat, onions and egg whites to a purée in a food processor or blender, let the mixture cool for 10 minutes. Add the chilled heavy cream to the chicken mixture in the food processor, a little at a time. Add the marjoram, nutmeg, salt and pepper. Grease 6 small molds or one large mold with remaining butter and fill with the chicken mousse; tap them on the counter several times to get any air bubbles out. Place the molds in a roasting pan half filled with hot water, cover with buttered greaseproof paper and bake for 40 minutes in a 300 degree oven. Meanwhile, cut out 6 pieces from one of the peppers (using a cookie cutter) and set aside. In a blender, liquefy the remaining peppers with the sour cream, season with salt pepper and paprika and warm slowly in a small pan. When ready turn out the molds on to warmed plates and decorate each one with a pepper "cutout." Pour the sauce over and garnish with watercress or parsley.

35

Serves 6.

Ash Hill Stud
Kilmallock
Co. Limerick

Potted Pheasant
with
Cumberland Sauce

36

** A little stock –
"Stock made from
pheasant carcass is
good, chicken stock is
fine, stock made from
bouillon cube is ok,
use enough stock to
moisten."*

*Susan Kellett,
Enniscoe House*

8 ounces cooked pheasant
1 onion, finely chopped
2 cloves garlic, crushed
4 ounces butter
1 tablespoon brandy
A little stock*
Salt and pepper
¼ teaspoon cinnamon and nutmeg

Mince or blend pheasant finely. Fry onion and garlic gently in 2-3 ounces of butter until soft. Mix into pheasant. Mix in the brandy and enough stock to moisten. Season the mixture with salt, pepper and the spices. Press into 8 ramekins. Melt remaining butter and pour a thin layer into each ramekin. Place in refrigerator.

Cumberland Sauce

(make sauce 24 hours before using)

2 oranges
2 lemons
16 ounces red current jelly
1 cup port
2 teaspoons arrowroot

37

Wash the oranges and lemons. Remove peel in thin strips from 1 orange and 1 lemon, and boil strips in water for 3 minutes. Drain and refresh, set aside. Squeeze juice of oranges and lemons into pan and add red current jelly, simmer for 5 minutes. Remove from the heat, add port and bring back to a boil. Mix arrowroot with a little cold water, add to pan and cook until the sauce thickens and clears. Add boiled peel. Keep sauce in the refrigerator. To serve slip knife around inside of ramekin, take potted pheasant out and place in the center of plates. Pour sauce around and decorate with more strips of orange peel.

Enniscoe House
Castlehill, Ballina
Co. Mayo

Sardine Pâte

38

2 tins of sardines in oil, drained
8 ounces light cream cheese, softened
1 clove garlic, crushed
1½ sticks butter
Salt and ground black pepper
Juice of 1 lemon
Chopped chives and parsley
Toast

Mix all ingredients except toast together in a blender and pour into a bowl. Place in refrigerator to set. Serve with toast.

Gaultier Lodge
Woodstown
Co. Waterford

Smoked Salmon Parcels

39

Cucumber
4 ounces smoked salmon, sliced
9 ounces crème fraiche
2 fresh limes
Fresh dill
Salad greens

Cut 4 slices of cucumber, place one slice each at the bottom of 4 ramekin dishes. Next line each ramekin dish with a slice of smoked salmon, ensuring plenty of overlap to fold over the top when stuffed. Put crème fraiche in a mixing bowl. Squeeze the juice of one lime into the bowl. Chop dill, add to bowl and mix. If you like you can finely chop a few bits of salmon and add to the mixture. Spoon the mixture into the ramekin dishes until about ¾ full. Fold salmon over the top so that edges meet in the center. Place in the fridge and chill overnight. To serve turn out parcels and place on plate with salad greens and fresh dill garnish with lime wedges.

Braeside Country House
Holywood
Co. Down

Snaffles Mousse

4⊕

8 ounces jellied consommé
(any consommé will do)
8-ounce package cream cheese, softened
Half clove of garlic
Pinch of curry powder
Dollop of lumpfish roe
Toast

Nicholas Tinne once owned a Dublin restaurant called Snaffles before becoming the owner of Emlaghmore Lodge. "Snaffles was frequented by everybody from pop stars to the diplomatique in the 1970's."

Nicholas Tinne

Blend jellied consommé, cream cheese, garlic and the curry powder in a food processor until smooth. Pour into 4 ramekins and place in the refrigerator to set. Garnish with a dollop of lumpfish roe and serve with toast.

Emlaghmore Lodge
Ballyconneely,
Connemara
Co. Galway

Smoked Salmon Pots

41

6-8-ounce package of smoked salmon (4 slices)
6-ounce can of tuna in sunflower oil, drain well
1 tablespoon cream cheese
1 tablespoon mayonnaise
1 teaspoon lemon juice
Lemon wedges, for garnish
Small amount of salad trimming
Melba toast, optional

Line 4 ramekin dishes with the smoked salmon. Mix the next four ingredients in a blender or mixer; until smooth. Divide the mixture between the 4 ramekins and fold the salmon over the top. Place in the refrigerator for 1 hour to firm up. Slide a flat knife around the outside of the salmon and turn upside down on serving plates. Garnish with a wedge of lemon and salad trimming of your choice. Serve with melba toast.

Fern Height
  Bed & Breakfast
Kenmare
Co. Kerry

42

Warm Salmon Mousse
with Lime Butter

9 ounces fresh salmon
1 shallot
½ cup cream
2 egg whites
2 ounces dried morille mushrooms

Preheat oven to 350 degrees. In blender liquidize the salmon with the shallot, add ¾ of the cream, the egg whites and continue to liquidize a little more. Soak the dried mushrooms in hot water. Take 6 ramekin dishes and grease and fill with half of the salmon mixture. Drain the mushrooms and cook with the remaining cream. Add the mushrooms to each of the ramekin dishes; fill with remaining salmon mousse. Place ramekins in a bain-marie and bake in the oven for 1 hour. When cooked remove from the ramekins and serve with Lime Butter.

Lime Butter

2 tablespoons butter
1 ounce cream
Juice of 3 limes

Cashel House Hotel
Cashel, Connemara
Co. Galway

Place all ingredients in a pot and boil for 1 minute.

Serves 6.

Limerick Salad

¼ cup Irish Mist Liqueur
¾ cup oil
¼ cup red wine vinegar
3 tablespoons Dijon mustard
2 tablespoons honey
6 small tomatoes, peeled and sliced
1 small red onion, thinly sliced
Mixed lettuce
Toasted sesame seeds

43

For dressing combine Irish Mist, oil, vinegar, mustard and honey. Set aside. To peel tomatoes drop into boiling water for 30 seconds. Remove and peel skin. Core tomatoes and cut into thin slices. Arrange tomato and onion slices on bed of lettuce. Spoon dressing over salad. Sprinkle with sesame seeds.

Serves 6.

Irish Mist Distillery
Tullamore
Co. Offaly

Southwestern Chicken Salad

2 cups McCann's Steel Cut Irish oatmeal
Boiling water, enough to cover toasted oatmeal
3 cups cubed, grilled chicken breast
½ cup diced red onion
¼ cup diced jicama
¼ cup diced yellow bell pepper
¼ cup diced green bell pepper
¼ cup fresh chopped cilantro
1 tablespoon minced garlic
1 tablespoon minced, pickled, jalapeño chiles
¼ cup mayonnaise (low fat if desired)
¼ cup sour cream
1 tablespoon fresh lime juice
1 tablespoon fresh orange juice
Salt and pepper to taste
Lettuce greens of your choice

Preheat oven to 300 degrees. Put oatmeal on a baking sheet, with sides, in preheated oven. Toast, stirring frequently, for about 20 minutes until lightly browned. Remove from oven and allow to cool. Place in a heatproof bowl. Cover with boiling water. Allow to sit for about 20 minutes or until just tender but not gummy. Drain off excess liquid. Place oats in a clean kitchen towel and tightly squeeze to remove any remaining moisture. Combine oatmeal, chicken, onion, jicama, peppers, cilantro, garlic and jalapeño in a mixing bowl. Whisk together mayonnaise and sour cream. Beat in lime and orange juice and stir into chicken mixture. Taste and adjust seasonings with salt and pepper. Cover and refrigerate for about 30 minutes to allow flavors to blend. Serve on a bed of lettuce.

45

Serves 6.

McCann's Irish Oatmeal
Sallins
Co. Kildare

Warm Chicken Salad

46

¼ head of iceberg lettuce, shredded
4 ounces of bacon, cut into strips*
2 chicken breasts, cut into ¼-inch strips
1 clove garlic, crushed
Soy sauce, small amount
Olive oil, small amount
½ cup cream
Seasonings of your choice
Garlic Croutons

Bacon in Ireland is similar to what we know as Canadian bacon.

Place the shredded lettuce on 4 serving dishes. Fry strips of bacon until crisp. Add the chicken strips and cook for 3 minutes. Add the garlic, soy sauce and olive oil cook for 1 minute. Add the cream and cook for 1 minute. Stir in seasonings. Spoon over iceberg lettuce and top with croutons.

Garlic Croutons

2 slices bread
Garlic butter

**The Grand Hotel
Tramore
Co. Waterford**

Cut bread into cubes and fry in garlic butter until golden brown.

Stuffed Tomatoes

47

**Small tomatoes, one per person
1 ounce bread crumbs
Small amount of melted fat, preferably
from cooking lamb
½ ounce finely-chopped mixed herbs
(parsley, mint, oregano)**

Preheat oven to 400 degrees. Cut tomatoes in half. Remove the seeds from the tomatoes, place seeds in small mixing bowl and mix bread crumbs in. Pour a small amount of fat into the mixture and add the mixed herbs. Fill scooped out tomatoes with the mixture. Place in the oven and bake for 20 minutes.

Rahan Lodge
Tullamore
Co. Offaly

Beetroot Supreme

48

½ cup balsamic vinegar
½ cup sugar
1 dessert spoon cornstarch
2 tablespoons finely-grated onion
3 or 4 small beets, cooked and diced
1 tablespoon butter (if serving hot)

*Meryl of
Martinstown House
states "Beetroot
Supreme is a firm
favorite even with
beetroot haters."*

Boil balsamic vinegar, sugar and cornstarch together for 3 minutes. Add onion to diced beets and pour balsamic vinegar mixture over. Leave standing 30 minutes or more. This dish can be served hot or cold. To serve hot add small pieces of butter and reheat gently.

Martinstown House
The Curragh
Co. Kildare

Soups
&
Stews

Carrot Soup

50

1 pound carrots
1 onion
¼ red pepper
2 tablespoons margarine
3 cups chicken stock
Salt and pepper
1 teaspoon coriander powder
1 bay leaf
Small amount of flour, for thickening
1 cup milk
Cream, for serving

*Sweat, a method of cooking vegetables in simmering butter.

Prepare and cut all vegetables into small pieces; put in a fairly large saucepan. Add margarine and sweat* over heat for 5 minutes. Add stock, seasonings and bay leaf and cook until vegetables are cooked through. Remove bay leaf, pour vegetable mixture into a blender and liquefy, add the flour and milk and cook for about 5 minutes until it thickens. Serve with a dash of cream.

Gortmor House
Carrick-on-Shannon
Co. Leitrim

Carrot & Orange Soup

51

1 tablespoon oil
1 onion, chopped
1 pound carrots, peeled and chopped
1 potato, peeled and chopped
1 tablespoon flour
3 cups homemade chicken stock
2 oranges, rind and juice
Salt and freshly-ground pepper
A little extra cream, for serving

Heat oil, add onion, carrots and potatoes and sauté gently. Cover with lid and sweat out for 5 minutes. Stir in flour and mix well. Add stock, orange juice, rind and salt and pepper. Cover and simmer until vegetables are tender. Liquidize in a food processor or blender. Return to pan. Serve in warm soup bowls with a swirl of cream.

"Carrig-Gorm"
Helen's Bay, Bangor
Co. Down

Chilled Apple & Apricot Soup

2 eating apples
2 ounces chopped, dried apricots
½ cup white wine
½ cup vegetable stock
A little grated root ginger
2 teaspoons sugar
Salt and pepper
⅓ cup cream
A few sprigs of fresh mint

Peel, core and slice the apples and place in a pot with the apricots, white wine, stock, ginger and sugar. Bring to a boil and simmer for 15-20 minutes or until fruit is soft. Pour mixture into blender and liquefy. Allow mixture to cool and add the cream. Serve chilled with sprigs of fresh mint.

Cashel House Hotel
Cashel, Connemara
Co. Galway

Grandma Murphy's Broccoli & Bleu Cheese Soup

53

1 onion, chopped
1 pound broccoli spears, chopped
1 large zucchini, chopped
1 large carrot, peeled and chopped
1 medium potato, peeled and chopped
2 tablespoons butter
1 ounce sunflower oil
8 cups vegetable stock or water, divided
Salt and pepper
3 ounces bleu cheese

Put onion, broccoli, zucchini, carrot, potato, butter, sunflower oil and stock or water into a large saucepan. Heat the ingredients for about 5 minutes, stirring well. Bring to a boil. Add salt and pepper to taste, cover the saucepan and simmer gently for 25-30 minutes. Strain the vegetables and retain the remainder of the liquid. Purée the vegetables in a food processor or blender. Return the puréed vegetables and the remainder of the liquid to the saucepan. Bring the soup back to a gentle boil and stir in the cheese until it melts. Care should be taken to ensure the soup does not boil quickly as this will make the cheese stringy.

Murphy Brewery
Cork

54

Homemade Carrot & Coriander Soup

1 onion, finely chopped
Small amount of vegetable oil
3 large potatoes, peeled and chopped
3 carrots, peeled and chopped
2 cups vegetable or fresh chicken stock
1 tablespoon coriander, finely chopped
Salt and pepper
Fresh coriander leaves (optional)

Sauté onion in oil over a low heat. Add potatoes and continue to cook over low heat. Add carrots. Finally add the vegetable or fresh chicken stock and simmer for 20 minutes. Add coriander. Blend in food processor until smooth. Season soup with salt and pepper and garnish with fresh coriander leaves if desired.

Rosturk Woods
Mulrany, Westport
Co. Mayo

55

My dear friends, Pat and Colette O'Carroll at the Famine Monument in Co. Mayo.

Ladywell Leek & Potato Soup

56

4 tablespoons butter, divided
2 leeks, chopped
1 small onion, finely chopped
¾ pound potatoes, peeled and chopped
2½ cups vegetable stock
Salt and pepper
1¼ cups Murphy's Irish Red Beer

Heat 2 tablespoons butter in a large saucepan, add the leeks and onion. Cook gently, stirring occasionally, for about 7 minutes. The leeks and onion should be soft but not brown. Add the potatoes to the leeks and onions in the saucepan. Stir occasionally for 2-3 minutes. Add the vegetable stock and bring to a boil. Cover the saucepan and simmer gently for 30-35 minutes, until the vegetables are very tender. Add the salt and pepper to taste. Add the remaining butter. Add the Murphy's Irish Red Beer. Simmer for 2 minutes. Serve.

Murphy Brewery
Cork

Onion & Guinness Soup

57

½ stick butter
14 ounces large white onions, sliced
5 ounces red onions, sliced
6 tablespoons all-purpose flour
4⅓ cups good beef stock
Bouquet garni
3 cups Guinness
Seasonings to taste
Crusty bread – baguette, for garnish
Clove of garlic, for garnish
6 ounces cheddar cheese, grated, for garnish

Melt butter in a heavy pan over a medium heat with the onions, until the onions start to caramelize and turn golden brown. This gives the soup its color. Add the flour and stir until the butter is absorbed – leave out or reduce the amount of flour for a lighter soup. Add the stock and then the bouquet garni for extra flavor. Simmer for 30-45 minutes, skim off any excess fat if necessary, now add the Guinness, simmer for 5-10 more minutes and adjust the seasoning as required. For the garnish slice the bread and toast on both sides. Rub one side with a clove of garlic, add the grated cheese and bake in the oven to melt the cheese. Ladle the soup into soup bowls, place the bread slice in the center and serve.

The Bushmills Inn
Bushmills
Co. Antrim

Roasted Carrots, Parsnips & Ginger Soup

58

* Grapeseed oil is a "hard to find" ingredient, I managed to find it at a food store that specializes in out-of-the-ordinary foods.

3 medium-size carrots, peeled and cut into chunks
3 medium-size parsnips, peeled and cut into chunks
4 ounces fresh ginger, peeled and cut into chunks
2 bay leaves
1 tablespoon chopped rosemary
3 tablespoons extra-virgin olive oil
1 medium-size onion, peeled and sliced
2 tablespoons grapeseed oil*
1 teaspoon garlic purée
3 quarts cold water
1 tablespoon vegetable bouillon paste or 2 to 3 cubes
Salt
White pepper, freshly ground
Herb croutons

St. Clerans
Craughwell
Co. Galway

Preheat oven to 360 degrees. Place carrots, parsnips, ginger and bay leaves in a baking tray. Sprinkle with rosemary and olive oil and roast in the oven for about 45 minutes or until well roasted. In a large saucepan, over high heat, sauté onion with grapeseed oil and garlic. Leave for about 5 minutes. Add roasted vegetables and cold water. Cover saucepan and bring to a boil, skim bubbles and add vegetable bouillon paste. Turn heat to medium and cook for about 45 minutes. In a blender liquidize the soup and pass through a medium fine sieve. Season to taste. Serve with herb croutons.

Thai Red Curry Soup

59

1 stick butter
1 carrot, peeled and chopped
1 onion, chopped
1 head of broccoli, chopped
½ head of cauliflower, chopped
2 vegetable or chicken stock cubes
1½ teaspoons Thai red curry paste
2 cups water
1 cup cream
Seasonings

In a large saucepan melt the butter and add all of the vegetables, fry on a gentle heat for 5 minutes. Dissolve stock cubes and curry paste in water and boil for 35 minutes. Blend vegetables and water with stock cubes and curry paste in blender. Pour mixture back into large saucepan add cream and seasoning, simmer until ready to serve.

Horetown House &
Cellar Restaurant
Foulkmills
Co. Wexford

Doyle's Fish Stew Provençal

1 leek
1 fennel bulb
½ head of celery
4 ounces salmon fillet
4 ounces monkfish
4 ounces cod fillets
1 pound mussels
4 ounces cockles
4½ cups fish stock
2 tablespoons butter
2 tablespoons olive oil
2 cloves garlic, chopped
1 teaspoon tomato purée
1 teaspoon chili powder
1 teaspoon paprika
Pinch of saffron
1 cup dry white wine
4 plum tomatoes, skinned and roughly chopped
Salt and pepper
Tabasco and Worcestershire sauce to taste
¼ cup Pernod (French liqueur)
Chopped dill and parsley to garnish

Trim and wash the vegetables and chop finely. Cut the fish into bite-sized pieces and set aside. Scrub the mussels and cockles, discarding any that do not snap closed when tapped; steam 1-2 minutes until the shells open. Remove mussels and cockles from pan and allow to cool, then remove the fish from their shells. Heat the fish stock. In a heavy pan melt the butter with the oil and garlic, adding the prepared vegetables after 2 minutes. Cover and cook gently for 5 minutes to soften without coloring, stirring occasionally. Add the tomato purée, chili powder, paprika and saffron, cook for 2 minutes, then add the wine and cook for 5 minutes, next add the chopped tomatoes, then pour in the fish stock and bring to a boil. Cook until the vegetables are tender. When the vegetables are soft, season with salt and pepper and add Tabasco and Worcestershire sauce to taste, then add a measure of Pernod. Add the chopped fish, mussels and cockles and cook 2-3 minutes or until the fish is just cooked. Sprinkle each serving with dill and parsley.

61

Doyle's Seafood Bar
  & Townhouse
Dingle
Co. Kerry

Irish Stew

62

3 pounds boneless lamb chops
1 tablespoon vegetable oil
3 large onions
4 large carrots, peeled
3¾ cups water
4 large potatoes, peeled and cut into chunks
1 large thyme sprig
1 tablespoon butter
1 tablespoon fresh, chopped parsley
Salt and ground black pepper

The Foxford Lodge caters to The National Museum of Country Life. The National Museum of Country Life is located in Castlebar, Co. Mayo and is well worth including on your itinerary.

Trim any fat from the lamb. Heat the oil in a large pan or Dutch oven and brown the meat on both sides, remove from pan and set aside. Cut the onions into quarters and thickly slice the carrots, place in pan and cook for 5 minutes until the onions are browned. Return the meat to the pan with the water and bring to a boil, reduce the heat, cover and simmer for 1 hour. Add the potatoes and thyme to the pan and cook 1 more hour. Turn the heat off for a while so that you can skim off excess fat. Pour into a clean pan and stir in the butter, parsley, salt and pepper. Serve with savoy cabbage if desired.

The Foxford Lodge
Foxford
Co. Mayo

On my first visit to The Museum of Country life I arrived on Bus Eireann, on a miserable, cold, rainy day. The bus had dropped me off on the side of the road at the back of the museum. I found myself climbing over a locked gate to get in. The bus driver promised to pick me up on his way back if he saw me standing on the side of the road. Needless to say, I climbed the gate a few hours later in order to catch my ride back to Westport.

The original estate house at The National Museum of Country Life in Castlebar, Co. Mayo.

Irish Stew

2 pounds mutton/lamb chops, cut into pieces
2 pounds potatoes, peeled
8 ounces onion, peeled and chopped
8 ounces carrots, washed, peeled and sliced
3 stalks celery, chopped
Salt and pepper
Mutton stock or water
1 tablespoon fresh parsley, chopped

Trim excess fat from chops. Brown meat pieces gently. Place a layer of potatoes in pan, followed by a layer of meat and vegetables and sprinkle with salt and pepper. Repeat layers finishing with potatoes. Add stock or water to cover. Cook, covered, over a very low heat about 1 hour or until meat is tender and vegetables are cooked. Serve sprinkled with fresh, chopped parsley.

Greenhill B&B
Ballina
Co. Mayo

Ulster Lamb Stew

65

1 leek
1¾ pounds potatoes, peeled and sliced
2 pounds cubed shoulder of lamb
2 large carrots, peeled and diced
½ small turnip, peeled and diced
1 large onion, roughly chopped
¼ cup pearl barley soup mix (optional)
Salt and black pepper
2 cups lamb stock

Preheat oven to 375 degrees. Cut green part off of leek, blanch, chop and set aside. Chop white part of leek. In a large casserole or Dutch oven, layer half of the potatoes, the cubed lamb, carrots, turnip, onion, white part of leek, pearl barley soup mix and rest of potatoes. Season to taste with salt and pepper. Pour the lamb stock over the top. Bring to a boil and place in oven for 2 hours until lamb is tender and potatoes are well cooked. Remove from the oven and sprinkle with blanched, green part of leek.

Grange Lodge
Moy, Dungannon
Co. Tyrone

Meats

Fillet of Beef

2 large baking potatoes, peeled and sliced
2 sticks butter
14 ounces beef fillet
10 cloves garlic
Olive oil
6 asparagus tips
4 shallots, finely diced
3½ ounces red wine
2 cups beef stock
3½ ounces shitake mushrooms, stalks removed
Tomato concasse*
Fresh tarragon
3-4 ounces foie gras*
Fresh herbs

67

*Tomato concasse —
Removing peel, core
and seeds from
tomato. Cut an X
on the bottom of the
tomato. Place the
tomato in boiling
water for a minute
or so. Remove from
boiling water and
place in ice water.
The peel, core and
seeds can be
removed by
squeezing the
tomato gently.*

Place potatoes in large frying pan with 1 stick of butter and fry until golden brown. Cover with water and greaseproof paper and cook until the water is evaporated and the potatoes are cooked. Pan-fry the beef until medium done. Place the garlic in a little olive oil and cook over a very gentle heat until soft. Cook asparagus in salted water. Sweat finely-diced shallots in ½ stick of butter, add the red wine and reduce by three quarters. Add the beef stock and reduce to sauce consistency. Slice mushrooms and fry in remaining butter. Add the tomato and tarragon to the jus. Place the potato in the center of the dinner plates and top with beef, mushrooms and the sealed foie gras. Place the asparagus and garlic around the plate and pour the sauce over. Garnish with fresh herbs.

*Foie gras is a fat-
ted liver, usually of
a goose; duck,
chicken or veal are
also used.*

The Killarney Park Hotel
Killarney
Co. Kerry

Serves 2.

Dublin Coddle

68

8 large pork or beef sausages (link type)
4 bacon rashers*
Small amount of oil
2 large onions, chopped
2 cloves garlic, crushed
4 medium old potatoes, peeled and cut into 1/8-slices
¼ teaspoon dried sage
Black pepper
¾ cup chicken stock
2 tablespoons parsley, chopped

** Bacon rasher –
bacon slice.*

Preheat oven to 350 degrees. Place sausages in a pan of water and bring to a boil. Reduce heat and simmer for 7 minutes, drain, cool and remove skin. Cut bacon into strips. Heat oil in a pan and cook bacon for 1 minute. Add onions and cook until golden. Add garlic and cook for 1 minute. Remove bacon, onions and garlic. Cook sausages on all sides until well browned. Arrange potato slices and sausage in a large casserole dish or Dutch oven, top with bacon, onions and garlic. Sprinkle sage and pepper on top and add chicken stock. Cook for 1 hour. Serve garnished with chopped parsley.

Sheridan Lodge
Listellick, Tralee
Co. Kerry

Liver in Cream Stout Sauce

1 tablespoon vegetable oil
1 teaspoon butter
1 pound calves or lamb's liver, thickly sliced
2 onions, peeled and sliced thinly
5 fluid ounces stout, Guinness or dark ale
2 tablespoons pine nuts
2 tablespoons parsley and thyme, mixed
8 fluid ounces cream
Salt
Freshly-ground black pepper
Bread slices fried in butter

Preheat oven to 250-300 degrees. Heat the oil and butter in a pan until barely smoking. Add liver and onion. Cook the liver briefly on both sides then remove liver only from the pan. Place the liver in a low oven to keep warm; don't overcook. Reduce the heat under the pan and cook the onions for about 5 more minutes until soft. Add the stout, pine nuts and herbs and let the liquid reduce slightly. Stir in the cream, taste and season accordingly. Return the liver to the pan and heat through. Serve on fried bread with sauce poured over.

Buttermilk Lodge
Guesthouse
Clifden, Connemara
Co. Galway

Braised Lamb Chops

Salt and pepper
1 ounce all-purpose flour
4 lean lamb chops
2 ounces butter or margarine
1 large onion, sliced
1 medium carrot, peeled and sliced
Large pinch of dried rosemary
1 cup white wine
4 ounces button mushrooms, sliced
1 teaspoon salt
8 ounces frozen peas

Mix a little salt and pepper with the flour. Trim all excess fat from the chops and coat well in the seasoned flour. Melt butter and brown chops on both sides, remove from pan and set aside. Fry the onion turning frequently until softened. Add the sliced carrot, rosemary and wine, stir well to mix in sediment from pan. Put chops, onion and carrot mixture into a covered casserole dish and cook for 40 minutes at 300 degrees. Add sliced mushrooms, salt and peas, mixing well. Adjust seasonings and cook for 15 more minutes or until meat is tender.

Greenhill
Bed & Breakfast
Ballina
Co. Mayo

Serves 2.

Honey Glazed Rack of Lamb & Parsnips

Rack of 3 lamb chops
Honey to pour over the top
Parsnips, peeled and cut into large chips
Mint sauce for serving

Stuffed Tomatoes on page 47 compliment this dish nicely.

Lamb rack should be trimmed. Pierce the fatty side of the rack with a skewer and pour honey over the top and refrigerate for at least 1 hour before cooking time. Preheat oven to 400 degrees and roast for 40-50 minutes, turning after 20 minutes and again for the last 10 minutes to crisp off the top. During the last 20 minutes of roasting time of lamb add the parsnips and generously coat them in the juices of the lamb and honey. Roast in oven until golden. Serve with mint sauce.

Rahan Lodge
Tullamore
Co. Offaly

Kilshanny Lamb Casserole

72

Kilshanny is a small town near the famous Cliffs of Moher. There is an abundance of wild hazelnuts growing in Kilshanny and a farm, which produces some of the finest Irish cheeses and yogurts. And, of course, the Burren lamb, famous for its tenderness. Hence, the name Kilshanny Lamb Casserole.

Potatoes, enough for 3-4 servings
12 lean, tender lamb cutlets
Small amount of cooking oil
1 onion, roughly chopped
½ pepper, roughly chopped (red or green)
1 small can of chopped tomatoes
1 clove garlic, chopped
6 basil leaves
1 sprig rosemary
½ pint light gravy
1 teaspoon fresh mint, chopped
Seasonings
Pinch of sugar
Yogurt for garnish
Hazelnuts, chopped for garnish
Grated hard cheese for garnish

Boil potatoes. Sear cutlets in a hot pan with a little oil. Add in vegetables and stir-fry for 1 minute. Add the rest of the ingredients and simmer for 15 minutes or longer, depending on how you like your lamb cooked. Divide chops into 3 or 4 large serving bowls. Put a generous dollop of yogurt on top, then chopped hazelnuts and grated cheese. Serve with some fresh boiled potatoes and soda bread.

73

We arrived at Temple Gate Hotel to a flurry of activity, an art fair at the hotel along with a party type atmosphere. The annual Ennis Trad Festival was in full swing. Live music could be enjoyed both day and night with more than 100 top class sessions at the pubs throughout town.

Temple Gate Hotel
Ennis
Co. Clare

Oven Roasted Rack of Lamb

74

**8 racks of boned and trimmed lamb,
seasoned and rubbed with garlic
Garlic, chopped
6 peeled potatoes, diced
8 ounces butter
2 tablespoons cream
Salt and pepper to taste**

Place lamb in a hot pan with a little oil and sear until golden brown on both sides and place in a 375 degree oven for approximately 15 minutes for pink lamb or longer for more well done lamb. Fry the chopped garlic in a little butter. While the lamb is cooking, cook diced potatoes in water to cover for 10-15 minute; add chopped fried garlic and cream to the cooked potato; season and mash. Remove the lamb from the oven and let rest for 3 minutes. Put garlic mash in centers of 2 warmed plates and cover with rack of lamb, drizzle pesto on top. Serve with warmed Killeen House Hotel's Salsa, page 32.

Serves 2.

Pesto

1 tablespoon fresh basil
2 cloves garlic, minced
2 tablespoons pine nuts
1 cup olive oil
1 cup grated Parmesan cheese
Seasonings

75

Combine all ingredients and blend to a smooth paste in a food processor and season.

Killeen House Hotel
Lakes of Killarney
Co. Kerry

Spring Lamb

6 lamb cutlets
Salt and pepper to taste
1 tablespoon olive oil
Red onion marmalade
Peach slices
Demi glace*
Pesto, enough to drizzle around outer edge of plates
Shiso cress*
Curly parsley, for garnish
Tomato emulstion*

76

Demi glace or demi-glaze, is a rich brown sauce or gravy.

Shiso cress can be replaced with mustard cress or water cress, as it is more for the presentation than the taste.

Tomato emulstion is a garnish that is formed to look like a flower. Using a sharp knife remove a wide strip of skin from a tomato and curl it around to form a flower.

Season lamb with salt and pepper and grill. Heat olive oil in a large frying pan, add onion marmalade, heat well, and add peaches and demi glace and mix. Strain off excess oil and arrange in center of 2 plates. Arrange 3 lamb cutlets (tepee style) around peach and marmalade mixture on each plate. Drizzle pesto around outer edge of lamb cutlets and sprinkle with shiso cress or curly parsley. Garnish with tomato emulstion.

Serves 2.

Red Onion Marmalade

1 red onion, thinly sliced
3 tablespoons red wine
1 tablespoon lemon juice
1 tablespoon brown sugar
1 tablespoon butter
Garlic clove, crushed

77

Put sliced onion and red wine in a small sauté pan and cook for a few minutes, until onion is soft. Add all other ingredients and simmer for a few minutes.

*Chef Mohammad is extremely dedicated to his cooking techniques as well as the presentation of his creations.
I would definitely be a regular customer of The Ould Murray Inn if I lived in Tipperary.*

Ould Murray Inn
Tipperary
Co. Tipperary

Baked Smoked Ham
with Cider and Pineapple Sauce

78

4 pound smoked ham, middle cut
½ cup cider
1 tablespoon mustard
1 tablespoon honey
¼ cup brown sugar
16 cloves
2 ounces cream
¼ fresh pineapple, peeled and diced

Place ham in a large pot with cold water to cover; bring to a boil then, pour out the water and refill pot with cold water for a second time. Bring to a boil again and simmer for 3-3½ hours. Preheat oven to 350 degrees. Remove ham from the water and remove the skin, score the fat in a diamond design. Place the ham in a baking pan and pour the cider over the ham. Spread the mustard, honey and brown sugar over the ham and stud with cloves. Bake in the oven for 30 minutes. Remove ham from the baking pan and keep warm. Add the cream to the juices in the pan and simmer for 15 minutes. Add fresh pineapple. Slice ham and serve with the pineapple cream sauce.

Cashel House Hotel
Cashel, Connemara
Co. Galway

Irish Farmhouse Bake

79

2 ounces butter
8 slices smoked back bacon, cut into pieces
1 large onion, finely chopped
4 ounces mushrooms, sliced
6 potatoes, peeled and boiled
½ cup heavy cream
4 ounces cheddar cheese, grated
1 tablespoon parsley, chopped
Salt and pepper to taste

You can change this recipe by replacing the bacon with 1 pound (cooked weight) of smoked fish of your choice.

Smoked back bacon is a hard to find item in the United States. I use Canadian brand ham sliced thick.

Melt butter and fry bacon until brown, remove from pan. Put onions and mushrooms in pan and cook until they start to turn brown. Cut boiled potatoes into wedges and arrange with fried bacon, mushrooms and onions in a baking dish. Pour cream over the top and cover with grated cheese, parsley, salt and pepper. Bake until golden on top rack of a 425 degree oven for 20-30 minutes, until crisp on the top.

Clougheast Castle
Carne
Co. Waterford

Drenagh Pheasant

1 stick butter, divided
4 ounces smoked bacon,
(similar to Canadian bacon), diced
2 onions
1 clove garlic, crushed
2 young pheasants
½ cup white wine
2½ tablespoons Armagnac (a brandy)
or Calvados (an apple brandy)
2 cups water
Bay leaf, thyme and parsley
4 ounces streaky bacon,
(similar to American bacon), crumbled
1 cup fresh white bread crumbs, to sprinkle on top
2 egg yolks, beaten
⅔ cup heavy cream
2½ tablespoons flour

Melt half the butter in a heavy casserole, add diced bacon and cook for 5 minutes. Slice and add 1 onion and the garlic. Cook gently until transparent. Remove onions and bacon from casserole dish and reserve. Sauté pheasants in the casserole dish, adding wine and more butter if necessary. Allow them to take color gently. Flame with Armagnac or Calvados and let bubble to reduce slightly. Return bacon and onions to casserole and add water, bay leaf, thyme and parsley. Turn heat low, cover and cook gently for about 45 minutes, turning birds over half way through. While birds are cooking, chop streaky bacon finely and fry until crisp. Add breadcrumbs and stir until brown, adding butter if necessary. Reserve. Remove pheasants from casserole, roughly shred meat and discard bones and skin. Place on a flat ovenproof dish and keep warm. Chop remaining onion and cook in remaining butter, stir in flour. Strain the stock from pheasants. Slowly add 1⅔ cups of stock to the onion mixture. Cook for 5 minutes and then strain, pressing onion hard against side of sieve. Reduce and skim, adding more stock as you do so – the sauce should by syrupy. Mix beaten egg yolks with heavy cream and flour. Add a little of the hot sauce, stir and pour back into the rest of the sauce. Do not allow sauce to boil. Sprinkle with bread crumb and bacon mixture, place under broiler until browned.

Streeve Hill
Limavady
Co. Londonderry

Irish Mistery Chicken

4 thin slices baked ham, cut in half
4 whole chicken breasts, split and boned
10¾-ounce can condensed cream of mushroom soup
1 cup sour cream
½ cup Irish Mist Liqueur
1 cup sliced, fresh mushrooms
Wild rice

Preheat oven to 300 degrees. In an 8x12-inch baking dish, arrange slices of ham. On each ham slice place a chicken breast, skin side up. Mix remaining ingredients and spoon over chicken, covering completely. Bake in a preheated oven for 1 hour, 30 minutes. Serve on a bed of wild rice, with sauce.

Serves 6-8.

Irish Mist
Tullamore
Co. Offaly

Snipe or Woodcock Casserole

14 breasts of snipe or 7 breasts of woodcock
½ pound sausages
Small amount of oil
6 potatoes
½ turnip
1 parsnip
4 artichokes, peeled
1 onion
½ cup pearl barley
Mixed herbs
4 cups red wine
2 cups chicken stock

May substitute quail for the snipe or woodcock.

If more wine and stock are needed the ratio is 2 parts wine to 1 part chicken stock.

Preheat oven to 325 degrees. Brown the breasts and sausages in a small amount of cooking oil in a Dutch oven. Peel and dice the vegetables and put into Dutch oven. Add the barley, herbs, seasonings and cover in red wine and chicken stock. Bake for 4 hours.

Temple House
Ballymote
Co. Sligo

84

My husband,
Bernard
Coleman
Pidgeon at the
entrance to St
Colman
Church.

Seafood

Fillet of Brill
with
Lakeshore Mustard Sauce

86

1 pound fillet of brill (perch may be substituted)
2 ounces fish stock or a dry white wine or a mix of both
2 ounces fresh cream
Salt and pepper to taste
1 ounce brunoise*of carrot, zucchini, or leek
(more for color than taste, but worth the effort)
1 heaped teaspoon Lakeshore Mustard
or another wholegrain mustard

*Brunoise – finely
diced or shredded
vegetables cooked
in butter or stock.*

Remove the skin from the fish (important, so the sauce will not contain scales). Bring the stock or wine and half of the cream to a boil in a nonstick pan large enough to hold the fish. Season; add the fish, bring to a simmer and cook for about 2 minutes then turn. Cover and cook a further 5-6 minutes, either on top of the stove or in a warm oven. Remove the fish and arrange on warm plates. At this stage the sauce should not be too thick – add more cream in stock if necessary. Now add the brunoise and the mustard and mix thoroughly. This process should only take about 1 minute. Cover half the fish and half the plate leaving the rest exposed. Garnish with a little greenery and serve immediately.

**King Sitric
Fish Restaurant
& Accomodation
Howth
Dublin**

Serves 2.

Dalriada Cullen Skink

6 shallots, finely diced
2 tablespoons butter
½ cup dry white wine
2 cups good fish stock
2 cups heavy cream
A few strands of saffron
2 skinless fillets of smoked haddock
12 boiled baby potatoes, peeled and sliced into thirds
1 bunch roughly-chopped spring onions
A few finely-chopped spring onions, for the garnish

For the fish cream sauté the shallots in the butter over a medium heat. Increase the heat and add the wine; reduce by about half (enough to drive off the alcohol). Add the stock and simmer gently until it has reduced by half. Finish by adding the cream and saffron and leave to thicken over a low heat. Cut the fillets in half and in a heavy bottom pan poach in the fish cream for 5-8 minutes, depending on their size. Meanwhile, sauté the potatoes in a little butter and toss with a scattering of scallions. Place 6-8 slices of potato in the center of a large soup plate then carefully lift out the haddock fillets and place on top. Spoon a little of the fish cream around the outside and sprinkle with the remaining spring onions.

The Bushmills Inn
Bushmills
Co. Antrim

Kilmokea Monkfish

88

Kilmokea is a wonderful 18thcentury rectory gracing 7 acres of beautiful sub-tropical gardens. Guests usually dine at one large dining table. Dining with other tourists for the breakfast meal is a great way to get feedback and suggestions on places to visit. Both my husband and I prefer the breakfast meal at one large table with other guests.

1½ pounds monkfish
Flour, seasoned with salt, black pepper and blackened Cajun seasoning
2 shallots, chopped
1-2 tablespoons butter
Salt and pepper
2 handfuls of chopped chives
1 cup fish stock
1 glass of champagne
½ cup of cream
Small amount of olive oil

Roll the monkfish in the seasoned flour and leave to stand. Sauté shallots in the butter, salt and pepper, and one handful of chopped chives. Add fish stock and champagne and reduce by half. Add the other handful of chopped chives and the cream and reduce by half again. Heat a frying pan until hot. Add a little olive oil and place the monkfish in the pan. Turn fish over after about 2 minutes. Cook for another 2 minutes. The monkfish should be firm when cooked, not hard. Pour the sauce onto the plates and place the monkfish on top. Garnish with chive flowers if desired.

Kilmokea
Great Island, Campile
Co. Wexford

Serves 4.

Italian Salmon Margaret Style

1 small onion, finely chopped
2 cloves of garlic, crushed
2 tablespoons olive oil, divided
2 chopped tomatoes or canned chopped tomatoes
2 small zucchini cut into small ¼ inch pieces
2 teaspoons oregano
Salt and pepper to taste
4 salmon fillets, 5 ounces each
2 ounces Parmesan cheese
2 ounces grated cheddar cheese

This recipe makes a grand (as they say in Ireland) presentation, and is quite easy to prepare.

Sauté onion and garlic with 1 tablespoon olive oil for 5 minutes then add the rest of the vegetables, seasonings and the remaining olive oil. Cook for 8-10 minutes then place the fish in a buttered dish. Top with the mixture of vegetables. Mix the two cheeses together and spread on top. Bake at 350 degrees for 20-25 minutes.

Serves 4.

Ballinkeele House
Enniscorthy
Co. Wexford

Oriental Salmon Pasta

9o

It was a dark, dreary night at the time my husband and I arrived at Murphy Brothers. Otherwise we would have sipped our dark beer and enjoyed dinner on the balcony watching River Moy go by.

10 ounces salmon fillets
2 teaspoons soy sauce
1 teaspoon stir-fry oil
10-15 cashews
½ onion, finely chopped
1-2 cloves garlic, minced
2 cups fresh broccoli florets
8-ounce package angel hair pasta
Watercress, parsley or chives for garnish

Cut the salmon into 1-inch strips and marinate in the soy sauce and stir-fry oil for ½ hour. Cook salmon on each side in a hot wok, remove from wok and keep warm, save the marinade. Roast the cashews and cut into smaller pieces. Stir-fry the onion, garlic and broccoli in a wok with a little oil for 5 minutes. Turn down heat and simmer with lid on. Cook the angel hair pasta according to package directions, drain and add to broccoli and onions in the wok. Add the marinade to the wok and mix in. Put pasta mixture on a serving plate and arrange the cooked salmon on top, sprinkle with cashews. Garnish with watercress, parsley or chives.

Murphy Brothers Bar
and Restaurant
Ballina
Co. Mayo

CLARE STREET, BALLINA, CO. MAYO.

~ ~ ~ ~ ~

SPECIALISING IN:
LIVE LOBSTER AND SHELL FISH.

~ ~ ~ ~ ~

Deliciously Irish

Wild Salmon
with Chive Sauce

92

1 cup white wine
2 tablespoons chopped shallots
½ cup cream
2 sticks butter
1 tablespoon chopped chives
Pepper
Lemon juice
4 salmon cutlets

Boil wine and shallots down to about 1 tablespoon, add cream and reduce again. Beat in butter in small pieces, keeping sauce just warm enough to absorb butter. Add chives, pepper and lemon juice to taste. Keep warm until service, (if it is too warm it will separate). Poach salmon in a small amount of water until just cooked. Place salmon on a plate and pour the sauce over the top.

Serves 4.

Enniscoe House
Castlehill, Ballina
Co. Mayo

Salmon Cakes

93

½ pound salmon, skin and bones removed
⅔ cup mashed potatoes
2 tablespoons butter, softened
1 egg yolk
Salt and pepper
Seasoned flour
1 egg, beaten
Bread crumbs, fine
Oil for frying
Pinch of chopped fresh fennel or 3 teaspoons fresh thyme
leaves and parsley mixed together

Flake the salmon and mix with the mashed potatoes, butter and egg yolk. Season to taste. Form into round cakes about 2 inches in diameter and 1 inch thick. Dip in flour, brush with beaten egg and roll in bread crumbs. The cakes may be kept chilled up to 24 hours. When ready to cook, fry in deep or shallow oil.

Ballymaloe House
Shanagarry, Midleton
Co. Cork

Feuillete of Fresh Scallops
with White Wine Sauce

94

4 ounces puff pastry (enough for eight 2x3-inch pieces)
½ cup white wine
½ cup fish stock
1 shallot, chopped
1 cup cream
4 tablespoons butter, cut into cubes
Salt and pepper
Lemon juice
1 pound fresh scallops, out of shell and cleaned
Small amount of butter

Preheat oven to 375 degrees. Cut pastry into eight 2x3-inch pieces. Place on a greased baking sheet and bake in the oven for 15-20 minutes, pastry pieces will rise, forming a pastry case. Keep warm until ready to use. Make white wine sauce as follows. Place wine, fish stock and chopped shallot in a pan, cook and reduce by half, add the cream and reduce again. Add the cubes of butter beating well. Season with salt and pepper and add the lemon juice. Sauté the scallops in small amount of butter for 5-7 minutes. Cut the tops off the pastry cases and set tops aside. Fill each pastry case with scallops and finish with white wine sauce. Place the tops on the pastry cases and serve.

Cashel House Hotel
Cashel, Connemara
Co. Galway

Serves 8.

Pan Seared Scallops
with Green Pea Puree, Black Pudding & Smoked Bacon Jus

95

6 scallops
7 ounces fresh peas
4 tablespoons butter
Salt and pepper
2 shallots
2 slices of smoked bacon (Canadian style)
3 cup red wine
14 ounces beef stock
6 slices black pudding*
Fresh chervil

* Black pudding is available in many Irish shops in the United States.

* Quenelles – tiny mousses poached in broth, then drained and served with a sauce.

Clean scallops and remove coral. Blanch peas, refresh in cold water and pass through a sieve, add 1 stick of butter and season. Finely dice the shallots and smoked bacon. Sauté in a little butter for 2 minutes, add the wine and reduce by half. Add the beef stock and reduce to sauce consistency. Grill the black pudding and remove the outer skin. Season scallops and place in a hot pan with a little butter, allow to caramelize on either side. Place black pudding slices between quenelles* of pea purée, not stacked but placed around a large dinner plate in a circle, and top each pudding slice with a scallop. Drizzle the sauce on top and garnish with some fresh chervil.

The Killarney Park Hotel
Killarney
Co. Kerry

Serves 2.

Pan-fried Scallops, Monkfish & Prawns
in a Coral Sauce

96

*Escallops are thin slices of meat or fish, without bones, gristle, or skin.

Aherne's Seafood Restaurant is housed in a beautiful building with gorgeous window boxes overflowing with purple and white flowers.

½ cup white wine

¼ cup cream

1 scallop coral puréed (the roe of the scallop puréed)

4 tablespoons butter

Freshly-ground black pepper

Lemon juice to taste

12 ounces monkfish, cut into escallops*

24 shrimp

8 scallops

Small amount of butter to fry scallops

Sprig of parsley or fennel

Place the wine in a heavy saucepan and cook to reduce by two-thirds. Add the cream and let thicken slightly. Pour in the scallop purée and whisk in the butter. Season with freshly-ground pepper and lemon juice. Steam the monkfish and shrimp. These will cook very quickly so you must have the sauce ready to serve. In a separate pan fry the scallops lightly in a small amount of butter. Pour the sauce onto the serving dish and arrange the monkfish, prawns and scallops on top. Decorate with a sprig of parsley or fennel.

97

Serves 4.

Aherne's
    Seafood Restaurant
       & Accomodation
Youghal
Co. Cork

Shrimp & Pasta

98

8 ounces shrimp, cooked
8 ounces tagliatelle pasta
½ cup fish velouté
Garlic butter, melted
3 ounces sun-dried tomatoes
8 ounces grated cheddar cheese
Fresh, chopped parsley

Cook shrimp and set aside. Cook and drain the pasta according to package directions. Put fish velouté in a small saucepan and bring to a boil. Toss the pasta and shrimp in melted garlic butter for 1-2 minutes. Add the fish velouté, which has been boiling, to the pasta and shrimp mixture. Add the sun-dried tomatoes. Place in serving dishes and sprinkle with cheddar cheese and parsley.

Serves 4.

Fish Velouté

Fish Velouté recipe from Viki Pidgeon

1 tablespoon butter
3 shallots, chopped
½ cup dry white wine
Heavy cream
Flour
1 tablespoon fresh basil

The Grand Hotel
Tramore
Co. Waterford

Melt butter and fry the chopped shallots until soft. Add the wine and reduce. Add the heavy cream and reduce again. Add the chopped basil.

Pan-fried Fillets of Turbot
with Fresh Crab Meat & Celery

99

2 large fillets of turbot or similar white flat fish
10 ounces fresh crab meat
1 green eating apple, peeled and finely diced
2 stalks celery, peeled and finely diced
Chopped chives, parsley and dill
Salt and pepper
4 tablespoons cream
2 tablespoons olive oil
Chopped tomato skin for garnish
Fresh parsley for garnish

Preheat oven to 375 degrees. Cut each fillet into 3 even slices for layering and season with salt and pepper. Combine crab meat, apple, celery and a pinch of herbs, season and blend in cream. Using a hot pan, sear each piece of fish but do not cook completely. Assemble the fish by layering the apple filling between each slice of fish using 3 pieces of fish per serving. Place in the oven for approximately 12 minutes. Warm olive oil gently and add rest of chopped herbs and tomato. When fish is cooked place on a warm plate and drizzle excess from baking tray onto fish. Spoon the warmed olive oil mixture onto fish and garnish with a sprig of fresh parsley.

Killeen House Hotel
Lakes of Killarney
Co. Kerry

Serves 2.

Pan-fried Fishcakes
with Lemon and Lime Mayonnaise

100

18 ounces fish, any type
4 slices white bread
¾ ounce mixed herbs
1-1½ tablespoons mayonnaise
½ lemon
½ lime
¼ teaspoon curry powder
Seasonings
Olive oil

Cook the fish under a pre-heated grill or in the oven for 5-10 minutes; cool and flake the fish into a bowl. Put bread into food processor and make into bread crumbs, adding herbs while still blending. Add the bread crumbs to fish and mix using a wooden spoon. Add mayonnaise, juice of ½ lemon and ½ lime, curry powder and seasonings, mix well. Pre-heat a frying pan with a little olive oil. Mold the fish mixture into 4 cakes and fry until golden brown.

Serves 4.

Horetown House &
Cellar Restaurant
Foulkmills
Co. Wexford

Desserts

Brownies with a Brogue

4 ounces unsweetened chocolate
2 sticks butter
¾ teaspoon black pepper
4 large eggs
1½ cups sugar
1½ teaspoons vanilla extract
½ cup Carolans Irish Cream
1⅓ cups flour, sifted
½ teaspoon salt
¼ teaspoon baking soda
1 cup chopped walnuts or sliced almonds

Preheat oven to 350 degrees. Line bottom of a 9 x 13-inch baking dish with cooking waxed paper. In a saucepan melt chocolate and butter with pepper on low heat. Beat eggs with sugar and vanilla until blended, and stir in cooled chocolate mixture, then Carolans Irish Cream. Sift flour, salt and baking soda into mixture and stir until blended. Add nuts. Turn into baking dish. Bake until pick inserted in center comes out clean, about 25 minutes. Do not over bake. Cut into squares or bars.

Carolans Irish Cream
Liqueur
Clonmel
Co. Tipperary

Queen Cakes

2 sticks margarine
1 cup sugar
4 eggs
2¾ cups flour

103

Preheat oven to 350 degrees. Cream the margarine and sugar together until it is soft and fluffy. Add 3 eggs, one at a time, and mix. After adding the third egg sift in some of the flour and beat well. Add the last egg and then fold in the rest of the flour. Beat well. Pour batter into muffin pans and bake for 25 minutes.

Makes 24 Queen Cakes.

Palm Grove Farmhouse
Castlemaine
Co. Kerrry

Caraway Seed Cake

104

½ cup sugar
1 stick margarine
1⅓ cups flour
2 eggs
1 teaspoon baking powder
2 teaspoons caraway seeds

Preheat oven to 325 degrees. Line an 8 inch loaf pan or an 8 inch round pan. Put all ingredients into bowl and mix well with an electric mixer. Pour into prepared pan and bake for 1 hour and 15 minutes.

Clarke's Bed & Breakfast
Kilrush
Co. Clare

Kerry Apple Cake

1½ sticks butter
¾ cup superfine sugar
2 eggs, beaten
1¾ cups self-rising flour
2 medium cooking apples, peeled, cored and chopped
1 teaspoon grated lemon rind
2 tablespoons demerara sugar
Pinch of cinnamon
Pinch of nutmeg
Whipped cream, for serving

105

Park Hotel Kenmare is an extra special place to me in that they were the first to share a few recipes with me for inclusion in Deliciously Irish.

Preheat oven to 350 degrees. Grease and line a 2-pound loaf pan. Cream butter and sugar together. Gradually add eggs and flour. Stir in apples and lemon rind. Pour into the pan and sprinkle with demerara sugar and spices. Bake for 1-1¼ hours. Serve warm with whipped cream.

Park Hotel Kenmare
Kenmare
Co. Kerry

Norebridge House

Bed & Breakfast

T.V., En-Suite Rooms.
River & Village View.

Inistioge, Co. Kilkenny.
Tel: (056) 58158/58117

Irish Fruit Cake

1 stick margarine
1 cup cold, strained tea
3½ ounces currents
2½ ounces golden sultans
2 ounces citrus peel
½ cup superfine sugar
1 tablespoon golden syrup*
2⅛ cups self-rising flour
1 teaspoon baking soda
Pinch of salt
½ teaspoon allspice
¼ teaspoon ground cinnamon
2 tablespoons demerara sugar

17

Golden syrup is not as hard to find as you may think. I found the golden syrup by the maple syrup.

Inistioge is a lovely, peaceful little town. Filming of the movie "Circle of Friends" took place in and around Inistioge.

Preheat oven to 350 degrees. Grease and line a 7-inch round cake pan. Put margarine, tea, fruit, peel, sugar and syrup in a saucepan and stir together over a medium-low heat until margarine has melted and the sugar has dissolved; let cool. Simmer for about 5 minutes. Cool. Sift the flour, baking soda, salt and spices together into a mixing bowl. Make a well in the center and pour in cooled fruit mixture and mix until well blended. Pour into prepared pan and sprinkle with demerara sugar. Bake on center rack of oven for 1 hour and 20 minutes or until cooked through. Turn out onto plate to cool. Slice and butter generously. This keeps well in an airtight tin.

Norebridge House
Inistioge
Co. Kilkenny

Pear and Ginger Upside-Down Cake

1¼ cups self-rising flour
2 teaspoons powdered ginger
4 tablespoons golden syrup
5 dates
4 barely-ripe pears
1 stick butter
½ cup superfine sugar
2 eggs
A little milk

Preheat oven to 350 degrees. Sift flour and ginger together and set aside. Grease an 8-inch round cake pan. Heat syrup; pour into the cake pan to cover the bottom of the pan. Cut 4 of the dates in half. Arrange the peeled, cored and halved pears in the syrup, place the date halves in the center of the pears and the whole date in the middle. Cream the butter and sugar together until light and fluffy. Beat in the eggs and stir in the sifted flour and ginger. Add a little milk to give a dropping consistency. Spread the mixture over the fruit and bake in oven for 45-55 minutes until golden brown and firm to the touch. Turn out onto a plate and serve with a ginger sauce.

Ginger Sauce

⅓ cup light brown sugar
2 ounces water
4 tablespoons preserved ginger, finely chopped
1 tablespoon lemon juice

Put sugar and water into a small saucepan and heat gently, stirring until sugar has dissolved. Bring to a boil without stirring until thick. Stir in ginger and lemon juice. Pour over pudding.

Temple House
Ballymote
Co. Sligo

Tipsy Cake

110

14 ounces dark chocolate, melted
2 sticks unsalted butter, melted
¼ cup water
⅓ cup brandy
⅓ cup whiskey
6 eggs, separated
1 cup superfine sugar
2 cups ground almonds
1 teaspoon allspice

My husband and I like flying into the Shannon Airport and more often than not we arrive totally exhausted around 6:00 to 6:30 A.M. It is quite difficult (not to mention scary) to be driving on the opposite side of the road from what we are used to, especially without a good nights sleep, so we choose to spend our first day and night in Galway. The Great Southern Hotel has a delicious carvery lunch and there are plenty of shops within walking distance.

Preheat oven to 325 degrees. Grease a deep 9-inch square cake pan. Line with waxed paper. Combine chocolate and unsalted butter, water and liqueurs in a large bowl. Stir until smooth. In a separate bowl beat egg yolks and sugar together to a thick pale color. Fold the egg yolk and sugar mixture into the chocolate and liqueur mixture. Mix in ground almonds. Beat egg whites until soft peaks form and fold into cake mixture. Pour mixture into prepared pan. Bake for 1 hour 15 minutes. Allow cake to set for 4 to 6 minutes before taking out of pan.

Chocolate Glaze

8-9 ounces dark chocolate, melted
1 cup heavy cream

111

Combine chocolate and cream in a bowl, stir until smooth. Refrigerate until glaze is thick and can be poured. Pour over cake. It is best to leave this cake in the pan overnight. Also do not slice for a few hours after pouring the glaze over the cake.

Great Southern Hotel
Galway
Co. Galway

Warm Chocolate Cake with Ice Cream and Strawberries

112

3 eggs
¾ cup superfine sugar
3 ounces dark chocolate (70% cocoa solids)
7 tablespoons butter
⅓ cup all-purpose flour
Vanilla ice cream
Strawberries

Preheat oven to 350 degrees. Beat the eggs and sugar together. Add melted chocolate and butter. Sift the flour and add to mixture. Take 4 molds (small round metal molds) and grease with butter and dust with flour. Pour the mixture into the molds until about ¾ full and bake for 8 minutes. When baked the center of the cakes should be soft and runny. Serve with vanilla ice cream and fresh strawberries.

Castle Murray House
Hotel & Restaurant
St. John's Point,
Dunkineely
Co. Donegal

Bushmills Irish Whiskey Cheesecake

6½ ounces butter
15 graham crackers, crushed
1½ cups whipping cream
2 cups confectioner's sugar
8 ounces cream cheese, softened
4 capfuls of Bushmills Irish Whiskey

This cake is served in the restaurant at The "Old Bushmills" Distillery.

Melt butter and mix with crushed graham crackers. Press mixture into the bottom of a 12-inch flan dish. Put in the refrigerator to chill while preparing the filling. Whip cream until soft and add confectioner's sugar. Whip cream cheese and add to mixture. Finally, pour whiskey into mixture and fold in. Pour filling into prepared flan dish. Put back into the refrigerator and chill until lightly set. Cut into slices and serve.

The "Old Bushmills"
  Distillery Co. Ltd.
Bushmills
Co. Antrim

Bailey's Irish Cream Cheesecake

114

A cute little lady by the name of Kathy Allen helped with breakfast in the morning. Kathy rode a little red moped to Clone House each morning.

¾ pound coconut or graham crackers
1½ sticks butter, melted
8 ounces cottage cheese
8 ounces cream cheese, softened
1 envelope unflavored gelatin
2 tablespoons cold water
Juice and grated rind of 2 lemons
6 tablespoons Bailey's Irish Cream Liqueur
1 cup whipping cream
2 egg whites
1 cup confectioner's sugar
2 ounces melted chocolate

To make crust combine coconut or crushed graham cracker crumbs with melted butter. Press into a springform pan and chill. To make filling, strain cottage cheese and mix with softened cream cheese; beat well. Mix gelatin with cold water, and let sit 5 minutes. Heat over hot water to dissolve, do not let boil. Blend water and gelatin mixture into cheese mixture. Add lemon juice and rind, and continue beating until mixture is very smooth. Beat in liqueur. Beat whipping cream and fold into cheese mixture. Beat egg whites until stiff; gradually add confectioner's sugar. Carefully fold egg whites into batter. Pour into crumb crust. Refrigerate 6 hours. To serve drizzle melted chocolate over top of cheesecake just befor serving. Additional liqueur may be added for more flavor.

Clone House
Ferns
Co. Wexford

Kathy Allen (pictured on the right)
along side her moped.

Bread and Butter Pudding

14 slices of white bread, crusts removed
6 tablespoons butter, softened
1 fresh nutmeg, grated or powdered nutmeg to taste
¾ cup raisins
2¼ cups cream
1⅛ cups milk
¾ cup sugar
5 eggs, beaten
1 teaspoon vanilla extract
Whipped cream for serving

Preheat oven to 350 degrees. Butter the bread and place a layer in a 10-inch baking dish, buttered side down. Sprinkle with a little nutmeg and raisins. Put a second layer of buttered bread in baking dish and sprinkle with nutmeg and raisins. Put a third layer of buttered bread in baking dish, butter side up and sprinkle with a little nutmeg. In a bowl whisk together cream, milk, sugar, eggs and vanilla. Pour over the bread, it may seem like too much, but it will soak in gradually. Leave for 4-6 hours. When ready to bake place dish with pudding in a roasting pan. Pour hot tap water into pan to go halfway up the sides of the dish. Cover the pan with aluminum foil and bake for 1 hour. Serve with whipped cream.

Delphi Lodge
Leenane
Co. Galway

Hazel's Irish Buttermilk Pudding

1 cup cream
½ cup superfine sugar
1 vanilla bean, slit in half lengthwise
1 package unflavored gelatin
(disolved in 4 tablespoons water)
2½ cups buttermilk
Soft fruit (optional)
Lemon sprigs (optional)

Scald half of the cream with the sugar and vanilla bean halves. Remove from the heat and allow the vanilla to infuse. Add the soaked gelatin to the warm cream and vanilla mixture; stir to dissolve. Lightly whisk the cream mixture into the buttermilk and allow mixture to cool. In the meanwhile whip the remaining cream. Then gently fold into the buttermilk mixture. Turn into a glass bowl and put in the refrigerator for at least 4 hours. Serve in small dessert bowls and garnish with fruit and lemon sprigs, if desired.

Assolas House
Kanturk
Co. Cork

Chocolate and Brandy Bread and Butter Pudding

*Castor sugar is what
is sold in the United
States as super fine
sugar.*

*Brioche is a sweet
light yeast bread.*

1 loaf brioche*
5 ounces dark high-quality chocolate (70 % cocoa solids)
6 tablespoons butter
½ cup brown castor sugar*
4 tablespoons brandy
1¾ cups heavy cream
3 large eggs
Heavy cream, well chilled for serving

Slice the brioche approximately ¼ inch thick and cut into triangles. Break the chocolate into squares; place the chocolate, butter, sugar, brandy and cream in top of double boiler over simmering
water. Once the butter and chocolate have melted and the sugar dissolved remove the pan from the heat and stir. In a separate bowl whisk
the eggs and then pour the chocolate and brandy mixture over them
and whisk again. Put about ½ inch layer of the chocolate mixture in
the bottom of a lightly-buttered 7 x 9-inch baking dish and arrange
half of the brioche slices over the chocolate in overlapping rows. Pour
half of the remaining chocolate mixture over the brioche as evenly as
possible and then arrange the remaining brioche triangles over that,
finishing off with a layer of chocolate. Gently press the brioche down
into the dish so that it gets covered evenly with the chocolate and

brandy mixture as it cools. Cover the dish with plastic wrap and allow to stand at room temperature until most of the chocolate and brandy mixture is absorbed into the brioche. Put it in the refrigerator until you want to bake it. When ready to bake, preheat the oven to 350 degrees.   Remove the plastic wrap and bake for 30-35 minutes. Remove pudding from oven and let stand for 10 minutes before serving with well-chilled heavy cream.

119

Lismore Castle
Lismore
Co Waterford

Ashley Park Lemon Tart

Flan Case

2½ cups all-purpose flour
¾ cup confectioner's sugar
1½ sticks butter
Grated zest of 1 lemon
Grains from vanilla pod or 1 teaspoon vanilla extract
1 egg

Preheat oven to 350 degrees. Grease a springform pan and line with waxed paper. Sift the flour and confectioner's sugar together and work in the butter. Make a well in the flour mixture and add the lemon zest and vanilla extract. Beat the egg and add to the well. Knead the mixture with your fingers, then wrap in plastic wrap and leave to rest for 30 minutes in the refrigerator. Roll out the flan on a lightly-floured surface to a size just large enough to fill the springform pan and fold the dough into it. Gently fit the dough into the corners and up the sides of the springform pan leaving about ½ inch overhang. Do not cut this off. Place a piece of waxed paper on top of the flan and fill with enough uncooked rice (about ½ inch) to ensure that sides as well as the base are weighted. Bake in the oven for 10 minutes. After 10 minutes remove the rice and waxed paper and trim the overhang from the flan. Return the flan to the oven and bake another 10 minutes.

Lemon Filling

121

9 eggs
1¾ cups superfine sugar
5 lemons (zest of 2 and juice of all 5)
1⅛ cups heavy cream

Whisk the eggs with the sugar and the lemon zest, reserving a small amount of sugar to sift over the top. Stir in the lemon juice and then fold in the cream. Remove any froth from the top of the mixture. Reduce oven temperature to 250 degrees. Pour the cold filling into the baked pastry shell. Bake at 250 degrees for 30 minutes. Remove from oven. Turn on the oven broiler. Sift the sugar over the tart as soon as it comes out of the oven and then flash it briefly under the grill to brown the sugar.

Ashley Park House
Nenagh
Co. Tipperary

Tarte Sablee au Chocolate

Pastry

7 tablespoons butter, softened
Pinch of salt
⅓ cup sugar
1 egg
1½ cups all-purpose flour

Preheat oven to 400 degrees. Mix butter, salt sugar, and egg in a bowl for 30 seconds. Add the flour and work into the mixture with a wooden spoon. Shape into a ball and cool for 2 hours in the refrigerator. Remove from the refrigerator and roll out the pastry and place in an 8-inch tart pan and cover with waxed paper. Cover the waxed paper with lentils and bake for 10-15 minutes in preheated oven.

Chocolate filling

123

5 ounces bitter dark high-quality chocolate (75% cocoa)
1 egg
2 egg yolks
1 ounce sugar
7 tablespoons butter, melted
Confectioner's sugar, for dusting
Caramel ice cream or whipped cream, for serving

Melt the chocolate slowly in the microwave. Whisk the egg, egg yolks and sugar for 2 minutes. Add the melted chocolate and butter. Pour into the tart and bake for 8-10 minutes at 400 degrees. Dust with confectioner's sugar and serve warm with caramel ice cream or whipped cream.

Restaurant Patrick
Guilbaud
Dublin 2

Ballyteigue House Quick Dessert

124

9-inch pieshell, unbaked
1 cup pecans
3 eggs
½ cup maple syrup
4 tablespoons butter, melted
Juice of 1 large orange
Grated rind of 1 large orange
½ cup less 1 tablespoon dark brown sugar

Preheat oven to 300 degrees. Put all ingredients (with the exception of the pieshell) into blender and blend a few seconds. Pour into pieshell and bake for 50-60 minutes.

Ballyteigue House
Rockhill, Bruree
Co. Limerick

Cardamon and Raspberry Roulade

1 teaspoon ground cardamon
1 cup all-purpose flour
3 eggs
⅓ cup superfine sugar
2 cups fresh raspberries
⅔ cup whipping cream
2 tablespoons superfine sugar, for filling

*Margaret Browne of Ballymakeigh House has a cookbook of her own, **Through my Kitchen Window.***

Preheat oven to 400 degrees. Line a Swiss roll pan with waxed paper. Add ground cardamon to flour. Whisk the eggs and sugar together until thick and creamy and holds a figure of 8 when the whisk is drawn over it. Very gently fold in the flour using a metal spoon. Pour the mixture into the lined Swiss roll pan. Level it off. Bake for about 14 minutes until the sponge feels springy. Turn the sponge out onto a sugar-coated sheet of waxed paper. Remove the lining paper and roll up the Swiss roll loosely. Meanwhile make the filling. Mash the raspberries to a soft pulp. Whip the cream. Add the raspberries and sugar to the whipped cream. Unroll the Swiss roll. Spread the cream mixture over it. Reroll carefully. Serve plain or with softly whipped cream.

Ballymakeigh House
Killeagh, Youghal
Co. Cork

Lemon Roulade

4 large eggs, separated
5 ounces curd cheese
5 ounces superfine sugar
Zest of 2 lemons
Juice of half a lemon
Confectioner's sugar, for dusting
1 cup whipped cream
Raspberries, to put over whipped cream
Raspberry Coulis

Preheat oven to 350 degrees. Line a 9-inch Swiss roll pan with nonstick paper. Beat egg yolks, curd cheese, sugar, lemon zest and lemon juice. Whisk the egg whites until they are stiff. Mix a spoonful of the stiff egg whites into the egg yolk mixture and then fold into the remaining egg whites. Pour mixture into Swiss roll pan and smooth gently. Bake at 350 degrees for approximately 25 minutes until firm to the touch and a light golden brown. Remove from the oven and cover with a damp, clean tea towel and leave to cool. Dust a large sheet of greaseproof paper with confectioner's sugar and tip cake onto it. Spread the whipped cream over the Swiss roll, put fruit over the whipped cream and roll up as a Swiss roll or any roulade. Serve with Raspberry Coulis.

Castle ffrench
Ballinamore
Co. Galway

Raspberry Coulis

3 cups raspberries, save ½ cup for garnish
¼ cup superfine sugar
1 teaspoon fresh lemon juice

127

Purée all ingredients together to make a thin sauce, saving ½ cup of raspberries for garnish.

Recipe by Viki Pidgeon

Lemon Soufflé

4 tablespoons cold water
2 envelopes (1/2 ounce) powdered unflavored gelatin
¾ cup superfine sugar
Grated rind and juice of 2 large lemons
Yolks of 3 eggs
1 cup cream
Whites of 4 eggs
Toasted slivered almonds

Put cold water into a small bowl, sprinkle on the gelatin and leave to go spongy. Put bowl into a saucepan of hot water and dissolve the gelatin until it becomes clear. Do not boil. Place the sugar, lemon rind and juice into a bowl over a saucepan of hot water and stir until the sugar has melted. Add the well-beaten egg yolks and melted gelatin. Pop into the refrigerator for about 15 minutes until the mixture starts to thicken, stirring occasionally. Whip the cream and add to the lemon mixture, and fold in the stiffly whisked egg whites. Pour into a glass bowl and leave in the refrigerator until ready to serve. Decorate with toasted slivered almonds.

Ballyvolane House
Castlelyons
Co. Cork

Irish Coffee

2 ounces good Irish whiskey
1 pot fresh, strong coffee
4 teaspoons sugar
¼ cup unsweetened whipping cream,
whipped to soft peaks (not too stiff)

130

Cregg Castle sounds like a wonderful place to spend some time. Ann Marie has quite a sense of humor. Her philosophy is that if the first Irish coffee you make looks cloudy "Just drink it yourself, after all, practice makes perfect! Then try making a second one that isn't so cloudy."

Place teaspoons in 2 large wine glasses (so glass will not crack) and fill the glasses with boiling water; pour water out. Pour 1 ounce of whiskey in each wine glass. Sweeten enough coffee for 2 servings with sugar and pour the sweetened coffee into the wine glasses within ¾ inch of the rim. Hold a spoon upside down so that the end of the spoon bowl barely touches the coffee (this will allow the cream to slide smoothly into the coffee). Spoon or pour the cream gently over the spoon so that it slides over the top of the coffee without dunking, and fill to the very top. The coffee should appear completely black and the cream completely white.

Serves 2.

Cregg Castle
Corandulla
Co. Galway

Christmas

Robin Hill House is located in Rushbrooke, Cobh, Co. Cork. and was featured in Ireland's Food & Wine Magazine. The write up included the menu for "Christmas Past," and Teresa Pielow was kind enough to share her special Christmas recipes. When planning your next Christmas dinner why not try something different from your traditional menu and sit down to "Christmas Past"?

Roast Goose Stuffed with Prunes and Apples
Served with Spiced Red Cabbage
Roast Root Vegetables
Boiled Parsley Potatoes

Serves 6-8.

Stuffed Goose

8-10 pound goose
Salt
Freshly-ground black pepper
2 onions, chopped
3-4 cups water
2 cups pitted and chopped prunes
4 apples, peeled, cored and diced
1-1½ cups fresh, coarse rye bread crumbs
2 tablespoons sugar
½ ounce flour

Twenty-four hours before roasting, rub the goose with the salt and pepper and refrigerate. Place the goose in a large saucepan with the onions and water and simmer, covered for 1 hour. Strain the stock and skim the fat and reserve. Keep stock and fat for vegetables. Rub the goose again with salt and pepper. Preheat the oven to 425 degrees. Combine the prunes, apples, bread crumbs, sugar, salt and pepper and stuff the cavity of the bird. Use skewers to hold the opening together. Place the goose breast side down on a rack in a roasting pan and bake for 45 minutes. Drain the fat from the roasting pan, increase the temperature to 475 degrees. Roast goose for 15 minutes or until the breast is golden brown. Remove the goose and keep warm. Skim off the fat from the roasting pan but leave the cooking juices in the roasting pan. Combine the flour with the reserved goose stock and add the mixture to the roasting pan. Slowly simmer until the sauce thickens. Season and serve with the goose.

Red Cabbage

1 red cabbage
4 Granny Smith apples
4 ounces red currant jelly
1 cinnamon stick
1 cup cider
½ bottle red wine
Salt and pepper

133

Cut cabbage into quarters and remove the center stem. Slice cabbage thinly as for coleslaw. Place in a baking dish with a lid. Peel and slice 4 apples and add to cabbage. Add red currant jelly and cinnamon stick. Pour over cider and red wine, season with salt and pepper and mix together. Cover with lid and bake in oven for 2 hours at 425 degrees. After 1 hour remove from oven and stir, cover and place back into oven for 1 hour.

Roast Root Vegetables

8 large carrots
6 parsnips
½ cup goose fat
Fresh rosemary sprig
Salt and pepper

Peel, top and tail the carrots and parsnips. Cut in half lengthways and quarter. Heat up roasting tray and add the goose fat. Place vegetables in tray add rosemary and seasonings. Place in oven at 400 degrees and roast until tender, approximately 40 minutes, turning vegetables to get an even color.

Boiled Parsley Potatoes

135

12 medium-size potatoes
4 cups retained goose stock
Salt and pepper
1 bunch parsley

Peel potatoes. Place in a large saucepan with the goose stock and onions (left from simmering goose in saucepan); make sure the potatoes are covered. Season and bring to a boil, turn heat down and simmer until cooked. Drain and place the potatoes and onions in a serving dish and sprinkle with chopped parsley.

Victor's Grandfather's Spiced Beef
Especially for Christmas

136

My husband and I viewed Lahinch Golf Course as we sat in the dining room during breakfast. Victor, the proprietor and owner of the Greenbrier Inn, personally handed me this recipe, his exact words were: "People have walked out of here with a lot of different things, but never a recipe." Victor suggests serving spiced beef hot or cold with horseradish and other relishes, such as cranberry sauce or red currant jelly.

The Greenbriar Inn
Lahinch
Co. Clare

6 pound beef brisket or silverside of beef
8 ounces salt
10 ounces brown sugar (unrefined)
¼ ounce saltpeter
1 ounce allspice
½ ounce cayenne
½ ounce cloves
½ ounce mace
Pinch of thyme
Bay leaves
2 ounces whole black pepper, ground
1 ounce juniper berries
½ cup molasses

Warm salt, sugar and all other spices together along with whole juniper berries and rub into meat really well. Stand meat in a bowl. Two days later add molasses. Turn carefully every day for 14 days (minimum). Tie meat up with cotton string before cooking. Boil 4-5 hours or until tender. Will keep 3-4 weeks in the refrigerator.

Margaret Daly's Christmas Pudding

½ pound bread crumbs
½ pound apples, cored and well chopped
½ pound butter or margarine
½ pound brown sugar
½ pound raisins
½ pound golden raisins
½ pound currants
8 eggs, well beaten
4 ounces candied mixed peel
2 nutmegs, grated
1 teaspoon cinnamon
1 small carrot, grated
2 tablespoons flour
Pinch of salt
2 tablespoons molasses
2 tablespoons of whiskey
Brandy butter

Make this pudding in November. Put all ingredients together except whiskey and brandy butter and mix well. Grease a large bowl, ceramic would be a good choice. Place a circle of waxed paper at the bottom of the bowl. Put pudding mixture into the bowl and cover with waxed paper. Place the bowl of pudding in a large pot of boiling water, water should be three fourths of the way up the bowl. Boil slowly for 6 hours. Check during cooking and add boiling water to the pot when required. After 6 hours remove the bowl of pudding, uncover and pour 2 tablespoons of whiskey over the pudding. Re-cover pudding with waxed paper and allow to become cold, store in a cool place. On Christmas day place bowl of pudding in pot of boiling water, boil for 1-2 hours. Remove bowl of pudding from pot and turn out onto a serving plate, remove the waxed paper. Pour a little whiskey on top and light. Serve with hot brandy butter and whipped cream.

138

Castle Salem
Rosscarbery
West Cork

Brandy Butter

4 ounces unsalted butter
4 ounces confectioner's sugar
8 tablespoons brandy

*My own Brandy
Butter recipe!*

Viki Pidgeon

In a small saucepan melt the butter; whisk in the sugar. Slowly add the brandy. Keep warm over a pan of hot water until ready to serve.

Contributors

Aherne's Seafood Restaurant & Accomodation, Youghal, Co. Cork
Ardeen B&B, Ramelton, Co. Donegal
Ash Hill Stud, Kilmallock, Co. Limerick
Ashley Park House, Nenagh, Co. Tipperary
Assolass House, Kanturk, Co. Cork
Ballinkeele House, Enniscorthy, Co. Wexford
Ballymakeigh House, Killeagh, Youghal, Co. Cork
Ballymaloe House, Shanagarry, Midleton, Co. Cork
Ballyteigue House, Rockhill, Bruree, Co. Limerick
Ballyvolane House, Castlelyons, Co. Cork
Braeside Country House, Holywood, Co. Down
Buttermilk Lodge Guesthouse, Clifden, Connemara, Co. Galway
Carolans Irish Cream Liqueur, Clonmel, Co. Tipperary
Carrigeen Castle, Cahir, Co. Tipperary
Carrig-Gorm, Helen's Bay, Bangor, Co. Down
Cashel House Hotel, Cashel, Connemara, Co. Galway
Castle ffrench, Ballinamore Bridge, Co. Galway
Castle Murray House Hotel & Restaurant, St. John's Point,
    Dunkineely, Co. Donegal
Castle Salem, Rosscarbery, Co. Cork
Clarke's Bed & Breakfast, Kilrush, Co. Clare
Cleevaun Country House, Milltown, Dingle, Co. Kerry
Clone House, Ferns, Co. Wexford
Clougheast Castle, Carne, Co. Waterford
Cregg Castle, Corandulla, Co. Galway
Delphi Lodge, Leenane, Co. Galway
Doyle's Seafood Bar & Townhouse, Dingle, Co. Kerry
Emlaghmore Lodge, Ballyconneely, Connemara, Co. Galway
Enniscoe House, Castlehill, Ballina, Co. Mayo
Fern Height Bed & Breakfast, Kenmare, Co. Kerry
Gaultier Lodge, Woodstown, Co. Waterford
Glebe Country House, Ballinadee, Bandon, Co. Cork
Gortmor House, Carrick-on-Shannon, Co. Leitrim
Grange Lodge, Moy, Dungannon, Co. Tyrone
Great Southern Hotel, Galway, Co. Galway

Deliciously Irish

Greenhill B&B, Ballina, Co. Mayo
Horetown House & Cellar Restaurant, Foulkmills, Co. Wexford
Irish Mist, Tullamore, Co. Offaly
Iskeroon, Bunavalla, Caherdaniel, Co. Kerry
Killeen House Hotel, Lakes of Killarney, Co. Kerry
Kilmokea, Great Island, Campile, Co. Wexford
King Sitric Fish Restaurant & Accomodation, Howth, Dublin
Lismore Castle, Lismore, Co. Waterford
Maria's Schoolhouse, Union Hall, West Cork
Martinstown House, The Curragh, Co. Kildare
McCann's Irish Oatmeal, Sallins, Co. Kildare
Murphy Brewery, Cork, Co. Cork
Murphy Brothers Bar and Restaurant, Ballina, Co. Mayo
Newpark House, Ennis, Co. Clare
Norebridge House, Inistioge, Co. Kilkenny
Old Weir Lodge, Killarney, Co. Kerry
Ould Murray Inn, Tipperary, Co. Tipperary
Palm Grove Farmhouse, Castlemaine, Co. Kerry
Park Hotel Kenmare, Kenmare, Co. Kerry
Rahan Lodge, Tullamore, Co. Offaly
Restaurant Patrick Guilbaud, Dublin 2
Riverville House, Tubrid, Kenmare, Co. Kerry
Robin Hill House, Rushbrooke, Cobh, Co. Cork
Rosturk Woods, Mulrany, Westport, Co. Mayo
Sea Shore Farm Guesthouse, Tubrid, Kenmare, Co. Kerry
Sheridan Lodge, Listellick, Tralee, Co. Kerry
St. Clerans, Craughwell, Co. Galway
Streeve Hill, Limavady, Co. Londonderry
Temple Gate Hotel, Ennis, Co. Clare
Temple Health Spa, Horseleap, Moate, Co. Westmeath
Temple House, Ballymote, Co. Sligo
The "Old Bushmills" Distillery Co. Ltd., Bushmills, Co. Antrim
The Bushmills Inn, Bushmills, Co. Antrim
The Foxford Lodge, Foxford, Co. Mayo
The Grand Hotel, Tramore, Co. Waterford
The Greenbriar Inn, Lahinch, Co Clare
The Killarney Park Hotel, Killarney, Co. Kerry
The Quay House, Clifden, Co. Galway
Zetland Country House Hotel, Cashel Bay, Connemara, Co. Galway

Index

Deliciously Irish

Desserts

142

Meats

143

Seafood

Starters, Salads, and Others

Deliciously Irish

144

Soups and Stews